Presented to:

_____

From:

_____

with Dr. David Jeremiah

© 2019 by Turning Point for God

P.O. Box 3838

San Diego, CA 92163

All Rights Reserved

Printed in the United States of America.

Answers to
Questions About
LIVING IN THE
LAST DAYS

DAVID JEREMIAH

Table of Contents

Introduction   1

Culture   5

Why is it important to understand the times we live in?   6

What lessons can we learn from men and women of faith in the Bible about living in our culture today?   8

What example did Jesus give us to fulfill our mission here on earth?   10

How is our world similar to that of biblical times?   12

Is any problem too big for God?   14

How do we find inner peace living in our world today?   16

How can I demonstrate the compassion of Christ in my interactions with others?   **18**

Practical steps: How do we live victoriously in times like these?   **20**

How can I be strong and fearless in my faith in today's world?   **22**

How should I respond to people who are hostile to the Gospel?   **25**

Why is walking by faith so difficult at times?   **27**

What signs of the Last Days are being fulfilled in our world today?   **30**

Is spiritual warfare real, and how do we prepare to fight spiritual battles?   **33**

Who is our enemy?   **37**

Circumstances 41

How should we respond to cultural pressures in our daily circumstances … job, neighborhood, friends, and family? **42**

How can the light of Jesus Christ brighten our life during dark seasons? **44**

What should I do when I don't have the answers to life's questions? **46**

How does God speak to us? **48**

How should I respond when I am feeling distracted by my circumstances? **50**

What should we do when we face persecution? **54**

What characteristics of God encourage us when it feels like the world is spinning out of control? **56**

What resolutions should I adopt to live my life for the Lord? **58**

What is a good way to measure the
state of my spiritual walk with God?   **61**

What is the best way to avoid spiritual
erosion?   **63**

What spiritual power leaks should I
watch out for?   **66**

How can I grow stronger as a person
of faith in the world today?   **68**

Conduct   71

What can I do to rekindle my love for the
Lord?   **72**

How can we counteract all the forces and
influences around us?   **74**

How can I develop a deeper prayer life
as I face the distractions of the world
today?   **76**

What steps can I take to overcome
my sin?   **78**

Where can I find the strength to live a godly life?   **80**

How can I live confidently as a Christian?   **82**

What will help me persevere during difficult times?   **84**

What are the benefits of remaining "cool under fire"?   **86**

How can I determine God's will for me?   **88**

What should I do to keep my mind under God's control?   **90**

How does our speech represent Christ to the world?   **92**

How am I to treat those around me who are hurting?   **94**

How can I encourage other followers of Christ?   **96**

What can I do to display Christ to those around me? 98

How can I be an influencer in today's world? 100

How can I maintain a calm spirit in times of trouble? 102

Company 105

How can I develop wise, godly friendships? 106

How can I leave a godly legacy for my family and friends? 109

As a Christian, how can I reach others with the Gospel? 110

What is the best way for me to invest my resources in the times we live in? 112

What are some ways I can express love and gratitude to those around me? 114

How can I live an authentic life
for Christ and be a witness to
those around me?   116

What are some principles for showing
grace to other Christians?   119

How can I be used by God in the
world I live in today?   122

How can I be a true friend?   .   124

How can I live selflessly as part of
the Body of Christ?   126

Commitment   129

I want Jesus to be more than a symbol
in my life; I want Him to be my Lord
and Savior. What is the first step I
should take?   130

What are some ways that I can
develop and keep an active faith?   132

When I don't understand the circumstances of my life or the world today, how can I discover God's sovereign plan for me? 138

How can I ensure that my faith is growing deeper and stronger? 141

Why is the hope for the world found only in the Gospel of Jesus Christ? 143

My walk with God seems to be at a standstill. What are the next steps I should take to draw closer to Him? 146

What is the first step toward trusting God with every aspect of my life? 149

Does God have a mission for each of His children? 152

In light of the world we live in today, should I have a personal mission statement of faith for my walk with God? 155

I know that God is the great Promise Keeper, but how can I claim His promises for my life? **158**

In the chaotic world we live in, how can I best share the peace that Jesus gives with people in my sphere of influence? **161**

Is there any event that would preclude Christ's soon return? **164**

How can I become a difference maker in the world we live in today? **167**

I want my life to be relevant—how can I put that into action? **169**

Commission **173**

What shall I do as I live in these ever-changing and challenging days? **174**

What are we to do as we wait for Christ's return? **177**

My desire is to stay dedicated to the
Word of God. How do I stay true to
that desire?   **179**

How does the Great Commission
apply to me?   **183**

Why is it important to study
prophecy?   **186**

Challenge   **191**

What should be my first step toward
living with an eternal perspective and
purpose?   **192**

I want to see revival in my world,
where does it begin?   **195**

Salvation Is for Today   **198**

Topical Index   **201**

Additional Resources   **204**

About David Jeremiah   **210**

Watch therefore, for you do not know what hour your Lord is coming. But know this, that if the master of the house had known what hour the thief would come, he would have watched and not allowed his house to be broken into. Therefore you also be ready, for the Son of Man is coming at an hour you do not expect.

MATTHEW 24:42-44

A little while longer and the world will see Me no more, but you will see Me. Because I live, you will live also.

JOHN 14:19

Introduction

The times we live in today may seem unique to our generation and culture, causing us to think that what we are experiencing only applies to today's Christian. But throughout history, Christians and the Church have experienced challenges from without and within. Knowing this truth gives us comfort and hope, but we are also not without answers for the questions that plague us today. In this book, we have posed questions that relate to our culture, our circumstances, our conduct, our company, our commitment, and our commission, followed by a concluding challenge for living successfully in these

Last Days. One theme that resonates throughout every answer in this book is that through Jesus we have hope for every circumstance and challenge we encounter in our life today. Jesus left us with a Guidebook that offers counsel on how to live in the "worst of times" as we look forward to the "best of times"—heaven with Him one day.

Discover answers to those nagging questions in your mind and resolve in your heart to live with optimism and hope for the future with this book, *Answers to Questions About Living in the Last Days.*

But know this, that in the last days perilous times will come: For men will be lovers of themselves, lovers of money, boasters, proud, blasphemers, disobedient to parents, unthankful, unholy, unloving, unforgiving, slanderers, without self-control, brutal, despisers of good, traitors, headstrong, haughty, lovers of pleasure rather than lovers of God, having a form of godliness but denying its power. And from such people turn away!

2 TIMOTHY 3:1-5

Culture

Why is it important to understand the times we live in?

Knowing God's plan for the future offers the ultimate source of comfort for today. His plan is located in the prophetic portions of God's Word, and can be found from Genesis to Revelation.

Prophecy tells us what's next in God's timetable—if we pay attention to the biblical signposts that are there for us to read. When we study prophecy, it teaches us to have conviction about how we live and to be courageous and to stand up amidst the spiritual, moral, personal, and political corruption of our day. When we are tempted to yield to the pressures of a corrupt culture, we can recall the heroes of the Bible who stood firm in their faith through trials.

Prophecy also comforts us in the midst of our chaotic world. As dark clouds begin to increase on the world horizon, our biblical hope for the future will be our lifeline. The Bible's divine insight tells us that God's plan for planet earth will be fulfilled: The righteous will be saved, the wicked will be punished, and the Messiah, King Jesus, will establish a kingdom over the whole earth.

Knowing God's plan for the future offers the ultimate source of comfort for today.

> **What lessons can we learn from men and women of faith in the Bible about living in our culture today?**

The biblical example of saints who have lived before us offers a road map for us to follow. They show us that we can, and should, live boldly, yet graciously, in a godless culture. It's not easy—it takes enormous courage, conviction, faith, endurance, and prayer. But there are ways we can stand up today as our biblical heroes did:

- We are to stand up for God by displaying faithfulness—honoring Him and His Word, day in and day out, as a reflection of His holiness.

- We are to be gracious in our attempt to influence a culture of ungodliness—showing restraint and respect to authority even when our Christian beliefs may conflict with their actions.

- We are to be vigilant—praying for God's intervention and guidance in matters we feel have gone beyond our control.

- We are to be steadfast—trusting in God and having unwavering faith and resolve that He is in control and will deliver the ultimate victory.

- We are to be strong—asking God for the strength, yet humility, to demonstrate His message to our culture in truth with grace, love, and compassion.

- Finally, we are to be consistent—changing our culture will not be a sprint, but a marathon.

> **What example did Jesus give us to fulfill our mission here on earth?**

The best way we can stand firm in our mission is by looking to the example of Jesus Christ. If you think it is complicated being a Christian today, the complexity of Jesus' environment was ten-fold compared to ours. How did Jesus navigate a path through all the competing parties and ideologies, and still remain faithful—even unto death? Jesus stayed on the message God had given Him through prayer, communion with the Father, teaching (witnessing), and meditation on the Old Testament prophecy.

He stayed true to His calling.

We can always ask ourselves, "Am I focused on my mission as a Christian? As a servant of Christ, do I commit myself each day to seek and follow His will and not my own?"

To best fulfill our mission while here on earth, we should follow the example and methods of Jesus:

- He was compassionate toward those around Him.

- He was connected to the people who needed God.

- He was committed to God's will.

- He was calm in the face of trouble because of His trust in the Father.

- He was clear with His message.

How is our world similar to that of biblical times?

Currently, our world is similar to the world God judged with the Flood, similar to the city of Nineveh before they repented, and similar to the Northern Kingdom of Israel under their wicked kings. There is great evil all around us—it appears to be the worst of times. Our world is falling into moral decay, just as many who lived in biblical days did. We don't need to catalog what makes these days some of the "worst of times"—our sins are evident even to the most degenerate among us. We have gone so far down the path of immorality that we are in the same league as Capernaum of old. If you remember, Jesus told that city it would go easier for Sodom in the day of judgment than for her (Matthew 11:23-24). While it may seem like we live in the worst of times, from God's prophetic perspective, the times couldn't be better. The very next thing that will happen on His prophetic calendar is the Rapture of the Church. The same words that allowed first-century saints to remain faithful in the worst of times will do the same for us: "Therefore, beloved, looking forward to these things, be diligent to be found by Him in peace, without spot and blameless" (2 Peter 3:14). "Therefore comfort one another with these words" (1 Thessalonians 4:18).

The worst of times always lead to the best of times for those who put their saving faith in the prophetic promises of God.

Is any problem too big for God?

Have you ever felt inadequate to deal with the problems in your life? Feeling overwhelmed, in your darkest days you may even wonder if God is listening to your prayers. In those moments it's important to remember: Our God is a problem-solving God and nothing is too big for Him to handle. He cares about your pain and He is not only listening, He is working on your behalf.

When asking God for relief and guidance, it is important to remember that He is sovereign God. Nothing is impossible for Him. Trust in His wisdom and His timing, for His ways and thoughts are not like ours (Isaiah 55:8-9). Have faith in His divine purpose and plan for your life. The Bible, Church history, no doubt your life, is filled with examples of how God has solved problems His way, in His time, according to His purposes. There is no problem too big for God!

Great is our Lord, and mighty in power; His understanding is infinite.

PSALM 147:5

How do we find inner peace living in our world today?

When King Ahaz and the nation of Judah were facing invasion by two enemies, the Lord gave this message through the prophet Isaiah: "Be careful, keep calm and don't be afraid. Do not lose heart because of these two smoldering stubs of firewood" (Isaiah 7:4, NIV).

Even earlier, Moses had told the Israelites by the Red Sea: "Don't be afraid. Just stand still .... The Lord himself will fight for you. Just stay calm" (Exodus 14:13-14, NLT).

This is a message for us: "Be careful ... keep calm ... don't lose heart ... stand still ... the Lord will fight for you." Do those words reverberate in your heart right now? The devil may try to invade your orbit and disrupt your day. The truth is we may have battles on multiple fronts because of the turbulent times we live in, but as we fix our thoughts on Jesus, we will be able to claim His perfect peace and persevere. Practice putting these three steps into action to find peace in your heart:

- Trust the Lord and do your duty.

- Keep calm and don't be afraid.

- Carry on and rely on God to fight for you.

Be careful. Keep calm. Don't lose heart. Stand still. The Lord will fight for you.

How can I demonstrate the compassion of Christ in my interactions with others?

The world can be a very harsh place. People are often unkind in their striving to make a place in this world, searching to find where they belong, or when they are asserting a particular point of view. The believer in Jesus Christ also has a point of view—a calling that we want to share. But we must share our beliefs in such a way that Christ is exemplified in our actions—by being calm and compassionate toward people. They won't be interested in the One we love until we show them His love and compassion.

When talking with people who are strident, we also need to be constructive in our discussions—and remain calm. Dealing with angry or unhappy people is not easy, but, again, when we stay focused and calm, we will be ready to meet the challenge.

Finally, we need to stay committed to our calling to be salt and light in this world we live in. We're living in the Last Days—in chaotic times—but, to quote from Isaiah, "In quietness and confidence shall be your strength" (Isaiah 30:15). As we await the Lord's return, your heart and mine should be comforted by this thought: Jesus said, "These things I have spoken to you, that in Me you may have peace" (John 16:33).

> *We must share our beliefs in such a way that Christ is exemplified in our actions.*

Practical steps: How do we live victoriously in times like these?

Every moment today is precious, not to be squandered or mishandled. As children of God, we should be wise stewards of our hours, redeeming the time, however disturbing and stressful the days may be. In Ephesians 5, Paul gives us practical steps on how to live in times like these:

- Be wakeful—awake to the times and our world—and live by shining God's light into the world.

- Walk circumspectly and guard our steps as we walk with the Lord.

- Redeem the time given to us, making the most of every opportunity.

- Understand the will of the Lord and ask Him daily, "Lord, what is Your will for me today? How can I serve you in ways large or small?"

- Be consistently filled with the Holy Spirit and commit yourself to serving Him.

- Sing, give thanks, and be humble—singing, gratitude, and submission are heavenly characteristics.

If you want to redeem the time in these evil days, begin by committing every minute of your day to live in God's will.

Therefore be imitators of God as dear children.

EPHESIANS 5:1

How can I be strong and fearless in my faith in today's world?

The phrase "Be strong" occurs about forty times in the Bible. The Lord expects us to claim the grace to keep this command. I want to give you some verses about this. Don't scan over them. Take the time to read each of these verses, maybe even aloud, so the full weight of these commands settles into your soul. I've listed them in the order they appear in Scripture.

- *Be strong and of good courage, do not fear nor be afraid … for the Lord your God, He is the One who goes with you. He will not leave you nor forsake you* (Deuteronomy 31:6).

- *Be strong and of good courage; do not be afraid, nor be dismayed, for the Lord your God is with you wherever you go* (Joshua 1:9).

- *Be strong and of good courage...for the Lord God—my God—will be with you. He will not leave you nor forsake you, until you have finished all the work for the service of the house of the Lord* (1 Chronicles 28:20).

- *Be strong and do not let your hands be weak, for your work shall be rewarded!* (2 Chronicles 15:7)

- *Be strong, do not fear! Behold, your God will come ... and save you* (Isaiah 35:4).

- *Be strong, yes, be strong!* (Daniel 10:19)

- *Be strong ... be strong ... be strong ... and work; for I am with you* (Haggai 2:4).

- *Watch, stand fast in the faith, be brave, be strong* (1 Corinthians 16:13).

- *Be strong in the Lord and in the power of His might* (Ephesians 6:10).

• *Be strong in the grace that is in Christ Jesus* (2 Timothy 2:1).

Do you think the Lord is trying to tell us something? The strength we need is available from the God we serve, and He gives us a commandment to receive it. He expects us to be strong in Him, in His power, in His promises, and in the grace of our Lord Jesus Christ. We must choose His strength to conquer our fear and live by faith.

> *The strength we need is available from the God we serve.*

How should I respond to people who are hostile to the Gospel?

Sadly, many people living the world today are opposed to the Gospel. So, how do we witness to those who do not want to hear it? In our world today, there is often a preconceived bias against anyone who believes in God, so many individuals are unwilling to listen to what we say.

I have a question for you: Does living your day-to-day life, when it seems you accomplished little, bear fruit for Christ and His kingdom? The answer is "Yes," if you were faithful to what God has called you to do. By your actions and your testimony, you are a witness at work and a godly influence to those in your life. Everything that is done by faith, even when we are unaware of our audience, will bear fruit for God.

So honor the Lord, even in the small things, and be a reflection of Him to others. They are watching you! When Jesus called us the salt of the earth, He was referring to our witness, our influence, our testimony. Satan hates it when his oppression becomes our pulpit and we are empowered to use our trials to further our witness for the Gospel. Scripture teaches that whenever God asks one of His servants to endure difficulty—which includes persecution—He intends it for His glory and for our ultimate good. Keep showing God's love in your life to anyone you meet—your life is a testimony of His love and grace.

> *When Jesus called us the salt of the earth, He was referring to our witness, our influence, our testimony.*

Why is walking by faith so difficult at times?

It's natural to trust in our instincts, our feelings, and our vision when we are in the dark. But we are called to walk by faith—to trust God when we can't see the path ahead of us. This isn't so difficult when everything in our life is uncomplicated and there are no problems ahead. But what about when the night comes? The dark, turbulent days are the most dangerous in the spiritual life. That is when our faith is truly challenged—when we must learn not to lean on our own understanding but lean on God's (Proverbs 3:5). The next time you are going through a turbulent time in your life, ask yourself: "Is this part of God's training for my spiritual life? Is this an opportunity for me to practice walking by faith instead of by sight?"

We know from the Scriptures that spiritual maturity is developed through instruction, and that instruction or training often comes through challenges and adversity.

- *Before I was afflicted I went astray, but now I keep Your word* (Psalm 119:67).

- *It is good for me that I have been afflicted, that I may learn Your statutes* (Psalm 119:71).

- *Unless Your law had been my delight, I would then have perished in my affliction* (Psalm 119:92).

If those words about training are not convincing enough, consider the training Jesus endured: "Though He was a Son, yet He learned obedience by the things which He suffered" (Hebrews 5:8). We often feel insecure when we can't see the light at the end of the tunnel. But we cannot trust our sight! Living by faith means we trust God above all else.

And if you can't see the reasons or the results immediately, don't worry. Trust Him. Why is such a simple idea sometimes so difficult to accomplish? Because it goes against human nature. We must train ourselves, with the help of the Spirit, to trust in God, daily, without wavering.

As you increase your faith through training, remember: "He *shall* direct your paths" (Proverbs 3:6, emphasis added). Step out in faith so God can direct you. God knows all the paths that your day and life will take. He is committed to guiding you through them all.

Trust in the Lord with all your heart, and lean not on your own understanding.

PROVERBS 3:5

What signs of the Last Days are being fulfilled in our world today?

Earthquakes are shaking, fires are raging, hurricanes are obliterating, tornadoes are spinning—humanitarian organizations today are often hard pressed to provide food to countries and cities affected by the destruction of natural disasters and their aftermath.

Sound like the evening news? Well, yes, but it also sounds like Matthew 24, the passage in which our Lord, sitting on the Mount of Olives, predicted the future of world history and the end of the age. Now, I believe the signs in Matthew 24:4-14 actually represent a description of the first half of the tribulation period. But these trends and events are not going to suddenly appear when the Rapture comes. They're going to increasingly characterize these Last Days leading up to the

Rapture of the Church, as they reverberate backward through time.

In our times, we see an increase of false Christs—not as people, but as growing trends such as fallacious spirituality, socialist philosophy, atheistic activists, and other similar ideas. There is also an increase of wars, famine and pestilence, persecution of Christians, lawlessness, and the weakening of Christian influence as a lukewarm Church limps its way through our modern culture. But this picture does have one bright spot— more people are preaching the Gospel in more places to more people than ever before in history! Our Lord doesn't want anyone to perish, but all to come to repentance. So we are His witnesses. These are exciting days! These are days when Israel is back in her rightful land, the signposts are speeding by, and the angel is warming his lips on the trumpet. As we see these things coming to pass, it means the Kingdom of Christ is drawing nearer.

We can almost hear the countdown. We're living in prophetic times and seeing prophecy fulfilled right before our eyes. It's time to look up, for our redemption draws near!

We're living in prophetic times and seeing prophecy fulfilled right before our eyes.

Is spiritual warfare real, and how do we prepare to fight spiritual battles?

Spiritual warfare is happening right now, and it is no less real than any battle ever fought between nations on the battlefields of the world. In fact, there is biblical evidence to suggest that the real battles in the universe are first spiritual, then physical (Daniel 10).

When you become a Christian, you join an army—God's army, the Church. The apostle Paul says that we do not fight our spiritual battles as the world fights its physical battles (2 Corinthians 10:3-6). We fight a spiritual enemy, Satan, who has schemes and strategies that he employs against us (2 Corinthians 2:11; Ephesians 6:11). Therefore, we must know our enemy, learn his identity, plans, and purpose, so we might stand firm against him. We must also keep our eyes focused on the Victor and our mind filled with His Word so we do not become entrapped by the devil's schemes. God intends for us to be "more than conquerors," (Romans 8:37) but we can't engage in spiritual warfare without spiritual weapons.

First, we must put on the full armor of God (Ephesians 6:10-18) and protect ourselves from Satan's forces. First Thessalonians 5:17 reminds us how we can win these battles— on our knees, praying to our Father. The most important tool we can utilize is prayer. Ephesians 6:18 instructs us on how to pray when encountering spiritual battles:

- Praying always (the persistence of our prayers)

- with all prayer (the possibilities of our prayers)

- and supplication (the petition of our prayers)

- in the Spirit, (the power behind our prayers)

- being watchful to this end (the precision of our prayers)

- with all perseverance (the perseverance of our prayers)

- and supplication for all the saints (and the purpose of our prayers).

The battle for our mind, our time, our heart, and our faith is real. We must claim the victory over Satan by putting on the whole armor of God—piece by piece—prayerfully preparing to triumph in Christ day by day.

> *We must know our enemy, learn his identity, plans, and purpose, so we might stand firm against him.*

You are of God, little children, and have overcome them, because He who is in you is greater than he who is in the world.

1 JOHN 4:4

Who is our enemy?

Once we identify our enemy, Satan, we must understand his personality and purpose. From the beginning in the Garden of Eden we see that Satan's nature is manifested by arrogance, pride, and rebellion against God (Isaiah 14:12-14). Though fallen, he remains a powerful creature on this earth and in the realm of heavenlies. Ephesians 2:2 calls him the "prince of the power of the air"—but we are not to fear Satan's power, only to recognize it. Just as a healthy recognition of electricity's power causes us to use appropriate protective measures, so acknowledging Satan's power makes us depend on Christ in whom we are safe. Satan is so powerful that he is able to hold men captive to do his bidding if they have not been freed from him by faith in Christ. The willful indulgence in sin on our part can give the devil's power a foothold in our life (Ephesians 4:26-27).

We must also understand Satan's purpose: Out of fury toward God, he will try to take as many of God's human creatures as he can with him to hell—that is his goal. The verbs used in the Bible to describe how purposeful he is in achieving his goals are these: he beguiles, seduces, opposes, resists, hinders, buffets, tempts, persecutes, deceives, and blasphemes. We must recognize his tactics to defend ourselves and those we love from him.

Remember, Satan is:

- The great liar and deceiver (John 8:44).

- The great divider, seen when he took a portion of heaven's angels with him in his rebellion against God (2 Peter 2:4; Jude 6).

- The great destroyer (Revelation 9:11)—he will destroy whatever he can: the Church, a life, a marriage, a ministry. It is his mission to break up and tear apart the work of God in this world.

We don't need to depend on our own bravery and strength to defeat Satan, but on that of Christ who is greater than the one who is in the world (1 John 4:4). And yet our faith and perseverance in battle *are* required.

> *Remaining faithful until the battle is over will allow us to see the ultimate defeat of our enemy.*

Circumstances

Be strong and of good courage, do not
fear nor be afraid ... for the Lord your
God, He is the One who goes with you.
He will not leave you nor forsake you.

DEUTERONOMY 31:6

How should we respond to cultural pressures in our daily circumstances ... job, neighborhood, friends, and family?

Cultural and societal pressures are real and powerful. Just the thought of an embarrassing or painful encounter with someone who opposes our faith and belief system can influence not only our actions but also, if we are not careful, what we believe. Overcoming the cultural pressures of our circumstances comes from knowing and trusting God's Word—by having a steadfast knowledge of who we are in Christ. There are four strategies that will encourage and strengthen anyone who is desiring to remain strong against the cultural pressures of our day and live a victorious life:

- *Renew your mind.* This principle is found in Romans 12:2. We renew our mind by continually meditating on the Word of

God. The world around us changes moment by moment, but the Word of God never does.

- *Reject fear.* What are the antidotes for fear? Fear is defeated as we embrace the power, love, and sound mind we have been given in Christ (2 Timothy 1:7). When those are present, we are inspired to trust God fearlessly.

- *Retreat into God.* When we are fearful or pressed upon from outside forces, turn to Him for courage.

- *Replace sight with faith.* Anxiety and fear about our circumstances can be replaced with joyful confidence as we walk by faith instead of by sight (2 Corinthians 5:7).

The antidote to the pressures of the world is to embrace and share the life-giving hope of the Gospel—it never fails, it never changes, it never fades—it is the hope of the world.

> How can the light of Jesus Christ
> brighten our life during dark seasons?

As you interact with people in your close
circle of friends and family, you will find that
everyone encounters difficulty at some point
in their life. There are unexpected illnesses,
chronic and untreatable diseases, financial
challenges, personal issues, and more. These
challenges can place a burden on our soul, and
if we aren't careful, life seems dark. How can
the light of Christ brighten our life at times
like that?

*First, rededicate yourself to Christ and enjoy
living in the light of His presence.* Make sure
He is the absolute Lord of your life. He wants
you to trust Him even with sickness, age,
and death—if He's been faithful to you in
the earlier seasons of life, He will not forsake
you now.

Second, spend more time in God's Word. Studying, understanding, and meditating on the Word of God is an important step in adding more of His light to your life. Examine His Word daily.

Third, let the light of Christ reflect from you to others. Find ways to serve Him. God can often use us powerfully during the darkest times. Take that time to pray, to write notes of encouragement, volunteer at church, and witness to friends.

> *Everyone encounters difficulty at some point in their life.*

What should I do when I don't have the answers to life's questions?

In life, there are times when we simply do not have all the answers. We know God has promised to work all things together for our good; but He did not promise to explain His actions or His timing, nor should He. We may not know the answers, but we can trust the One who does. This truth helps us grow in our faith—trusting purely in the sufficiency of God's grace even when we don't know what's next and when our prayers seem unanswered. We have to recognize that we may never know all the answers, at least not on earth. We need to learn to say, "I don't know, and that's okay." There's something liberating about admitting we have no answers, and we can be all right with that. Our mind isn't always big enough to understand His unsearchable ways. And that's okay.

We may not know the answers, but we can trust the One who does.

How does God speak to us?

The first and most apparent way God speaks to us is through His Word. God has made it abundantly possible for us to hear Him through the study of His Word. Psalm 19:7-9 says that the Word of God is perfect, sure, right, pure, clean, true, and righteous. The first place we should turn to hear God speak is through His Word.

God also speaks to us through others. He intends for the Body of Christ to be able to minister to itself through its members helping and advising one another. But remember: When we seek counsel from other people, such counsel must be evaluated against Scripture. Be open to God speaking through others in your life. The more we surround ourselves with godly friends, mentors, and counselors, the more likely we will be able to hear God's voice.

God also speaks through circumstances. Time and again, we can detect God's guidance, receive His grace, understand His will, and hear His voice through the circumstances He arranges or allows. The Bible is filled with stories of God using "happenings" to speak to His people. We must remember our disappointments may be His appointments, and behind every "happening" is the hidden hand of heaven.

Finally, God speaks to us through silence. Our world is blanketed by so much noise that our souls are chronically stressed. We must be careful not to tune out God—only one thing will overcome the clamor of culture, and that's the silence of meditating on God's Word. In our loud world, we need to be still enough to hear and quiet enough to enjoy His presence.

> **How should I respond when I am feeling distracted by my circumstances?**

One of the worst train accidents in American history happened in the fall of 2008 near Chatsworth, California. A Metrolink commuter train ran a red light on the tracks and collided head-on with a freight train, killing 25 people and injuring 135 others. So what went wrong? When investigators probed the accident, they found that the engineer received seven text messages and had sent five himself during that fateful ride. It is amazing to think that something as simple as a cell phone could be so distracting to a veteran engineer that it cost so many people their lives, including the engineer himself. But that is what distractions do—they can trip up the most competent and experienced people and wreak havoc in all manner of ways.

Distractions can also lead us away from our relationship with God. And it does not even matter what the distraction is—for good, bad, or indifferent, anything that takes our attention off of the Savior is a hindrance to our spiritual walk. The distraction may be worldly or it could be worthy, and it could still have the effect of taking our eyes off the Lord.

Although advances in technology, science, and medicine have largely changed the way we live our life in the twenty-first century, the allure of sin in this world has not changed its shape at all. Power and wealth are the main detractors and enticers of the world today, and that is how it was when God's Word was being written. We are reminded of this truth in 1 John 2:15-17:

Do not love the world or the things in the world. If anyone loves the world, the love of the Father is not in him. For all that is in the world—the lust of the flesh, the lust of the eyes, and the pride of life—is not of the Father but is of the world. And the world is passing away, and the lust of it; but he who does the will of God abides forever.

It is also possible to become so caught up in serving God and working for His kingdom that we neglect the One for whom we are working. But, if we stay rooted in Christ in all that we do, neither worldly nor worthy distractions will draw us away from His side.

As you therefore have received Christ Jesus the Lord, so walk in Him, rooted and built up in Him and established in the faith, as you have been taught, abounding in it with thanksgiving.

COLOSSIANS 2:6-7

What should we do when we face persecution?

If you are an outspoken child of God today, you may find yourself facing persecution from unbelievers. As Christians, the nature of our Christian faith makes us a target for the devil. We must prepare for these attacks and trust in the One who is on our side. God has not promised to keep us from difficulty, but to be with us in it—caring for us and encouraging us through any persecution we might face. Many of our biblical heroes faced persecution—Daniel, Elijah, Noah, Stephen, Paul, and our own Lord Jesus, among many others. Remember them and imitate their example. Like our biblical heroes, we can't change our convictions so people will like us. During distress and trouble, trust God. Neither the devil, nor the people against us, know what to do with people who refuse to be intimidated and stand strong in their faith.

We can't change our convictions so people will like us.

> **What characteristics of God encourage us when it feels like the world is spinning out of control?**

When the world causes others to tremble and be overcome with fear, we can live with confidence because we know that God is in control. Fully understanding who God is encourages us in unsure times.

Remember these characteristics of our loving God:

- God is eternal—nothing surprises Him, for He sees all of eternity at once (Psalm 90:2).

- God is sovereign—every human decision is subject to the sovereign will of God.

- God is mindful and merciful—He doesn't turn away from the problems of His creation but works all things together for His purpose (Romans 8:28-29).

- God has a plan—God's relation to humanity is like a potter to His clay; He lovingly and righteously shapes human history for His glory (Jeremiah 18:1-10).

- God is everywhere present—there is no crisis, eruption, calamity, or need that occurs outside of God's awareness.

- He is unchanging—He has one never-changing story: the story of redemption.

- God is wise—He never labors to decide how to solve a world crisis because "His understanding is infinite" (Psalm 147:4-6).

Whenever it feels as if the world is out of control—remember Who is in control.

What resolutions should I adopt to live my life for the Lord?

First, evaluate areas in your life that need improvement. Be honest with yourself about areas that need attention.

- First, don't procrastinate. Get started today.

- Second, ask God to show you what to do. For believers, this kind of self-evaluation leads to prayer. Ask God for help and guidance.

- Third, develop a strategy. Schedule some time for an appointment with yourself. Write down changes to implement in your life. Plan for how you can purposefully grow in these areas.

- Fourth, adopt the changes onto your calendar, for change usually requires modification in your daily regimen. It takes both time and time management to change a pattern in life.

- Fifth, memorize selected Bible verses. Only the words of Scripture are powerful enough to bring change to our life! Only by hiding God's Word in our heart can we avoid sinning against the Lord.

- Sixth, recruit reinforcements. Surround yourself with friends and fellow believers who will strengthen your faith.

Finally, don't give up. Change is often difficult to sustain. So, ask God for guidance, direction, and strength to persevere and press on to victory.

But the fruit of the Spirit is love, joy, peace, longsuffering, kindness, goodness, faithfulness, gentleness, self-control.

GALATIANS 5:22-23

> **What is a good way to measure the state of my spiritual walk with God?**

We examine almost every other part of our life more than we examine our spiritual life. One simple way to examine the state of our spiritual life is by comparing it to the simple list in Galatians 5:22-23—the fruit of the Spirit. Ask yourself the following questions:

Do I *love* others unconditionally?

Am I able to *rejoice* in every circumstance?

Can I make it through a difficult circumstance without worrying because of my inner *peace*?

How often do I react impulsively instead of responding *patiently*?

Are my thoughts and words toward others *kind*?

Am I *good* to others? Am I loyal and *faithful* to God and others?

Am I ever harsh, unyielding, or insistent on my interests, or do I practice *gentleness*?

Do I have *self-control* as I live out my life, or am I subject to the desires of my flesh?

Signposts that we are living a balanced and healthy spiritual life are: joyful contentment, growth in Christlikeness, increasing knowledge of Scripture, service for Christ, a vibrant, up-to-date testimony, and fruitful, biblically-based relationships with family and friends.

What is the best way to avoid spiritual erosion?

When the influences of the world begin to seep into the Christian's habits or heart, they can create unseen spiritual erosion. On the outside, everything seems fine—but worldly influences have a way of silently eroding foundations. The collapse may seem sudden, but the destructive seepage was gradual. To avoid spiritual erosion, there are a few questions we can ask ourselves to examine where spiritual rust may be taking a hold.

Ask yourself:

How much television do I watch every day? While some programs are relatively harmless, some are downright harmful, and watching them is like taking a glass-bottom boat ride through the sewers.

How much time do I spend idly surfing the Internet? While it is a helpful tool for research and keeping up with friends, it can also be a huge sinkhole swallowing up vast amounts of time and sanctity.

What am I reading? It's all right to enjoy leisure reading, and the right novels are restful and entertaining—but remember that our reading material is our mental diet, and whatever we feed our mind will influence who we are. We must choose carefully.

How much time do I spend each day soaking up the endless flow of news and commentary offered by various political or media outlets? We all have our political viewpoints, and the media has learned how to stoke our boilers. Don't allow the continuous cycle of news and commentary to distract you from what is good and blessed.

Are my friends the kind who draw me closer to the Lord or do they tend to weaken my Christian zeal?

Who we surround ourselves with will have an effect on who we are.

Is there anything on my computer I'd be ashamed to show Jesus? Philippians 4:8 tells us to saturate our mind with what is true, noble, just, pure, lovely, and of good report. We sometimes need to turn off the constant streams of noise and distraction so we'll have time to meditate on the things of God and allow His Word to seep into our conscious, subconscious, and unconscious thoughts.

> *Remember that our reading material is our mental diet, and whatever we feed our mind will influence who we are. We must choose carefully.*

What spiritual power leaks should I watch out for?

The New Testament speaks clearly of at least two ways Christians can lose spiritual power and resources: *grieving* the Spirit (Ephesians 4:30) and *quenching* the Spirit (1 Thessalonians 5:19). Here are four ways that spiritual power drains out of our life as our choices negate the work of the Spirit in us:

The drain of negative influence—inappropriate friendships and relationships can lead us away from God (Deuteronomy 13:6-9), impact our character and behavior (Proverbs 22:24-25), and cause us to become an enemy of God (James 4:4).

The drain of busyness—spiritual growth and power take time and effort. Yes, the Holy Spirit does the changing in us, but we make ourselves available to Him through the spiritual disciplines of prayer, Bible study, worship, service, fellowship, meditation on Scripture, and others.

The drain of materialism—Matthew 6:24 says, "No one can serve two masters .... You cannot serve God and mammon." In modern terms, this means we cannot serve God wholeheartedly if our spiritual power is being drained away in the pursuit of materialism.

The drain of envy or jealousy—Proverbs 14:30 says that "envy is rottenness to the bones." That is not a life where spiritual power is being stored up, so we must avoid the temptations to envy and compare ourselves to others.

There are other spiritual drains, but these represent tiny leaks that, over time, allow our spiritual power to dissipate and vanish.

How can I grow stronger as a person of faith in the world today?

You are not alone if you feel you are the only one who ever experienced a crisis of faith. For some people this occurs when they are physically tired or burdened by the cares of daily living in our world today. Whatever the cause or the circumstance, when you feel weak, you need to remember that God is faithful—even when we are faithless (2 Timothy 2:13). But how do we do this?

First, we must seek God—and not only in a moment of crisis, but daily. The best time to prepare for trials is before we face them. Our faith *will* be tested. We must seek God now.

Second, we have to obey God—another ongoing discipline. We have to trust Him where He leads us and practice saying, "Lord, I yield my understanding to Yours."

Third, we need to acknowledge everything that is true—admitting fear and apprehension is not sin. What *is* sin is elevating our weakness above God's strength. We must acknowledge who He is and acknowledge how we feel. Talk to Him and remember to give His promises a higher priority than your fears.

Fourth, we have to respond to God—take everything we've learned and act on it. Like Mary, the mother of Jesus, we should say, "Let it be to me according to your word" (Luke 1:38).

If we are faithless,
He remains faithful;
He cannot deny Himself.

2 TIMOTHY 2:13

Conduct

And the grace of our Lord was exceedingly abundant, with faith and love which are in Christ Jesus. This is a faithful saying and worthy of all acceptance, that Christ Jesus came into the world to save sinners, of whom I am chief.

1 TIMOTHY 1:14-15

What can I do to rekindle my love for the Lord?

Revelation 2:5 says, "Remember therefore from where you have fallen; repent and do the first works." In this verse, Jesus gives a simple formula for rekindling your love for Him: remember, repent, renew.

First, remember when you met Christ. Remember the exuberance you experienced when He

Wake up every morning with a commitment to fufill His will for your life that day.

saved you by His own suffering and when you discovered eternal life. Remember how wonderful it felt to walk in fellowship with Him through daily time in His Word and continual prayer.

Second, repent of allowing your love to grow cold. Sometimes you might allow busyness to erode your love. Sometimes it's bitterness. Sometimes it's a lost battle with sinful tendencies. Whatever the cause, you can't correct it without expressing your sorrow and sin to God.

Third, renew your commitment to Him. Rededicate yourself to worshiping Him, walking with Him, and working for Him. Rediscover His purpose for your life and wake up every morning with a commitment to fulfill His will for your life that day. Return to reading Scripture each day and spending time talking with Him in prayer.

> **How can we counteract all the forces and influences around us?**

The influence of the Internet on our life is profound, and the numerous opportunities to waste our time and our thoughts on ungodly sites or meaningless material are real. How can we counteract all the forces and influences around us? The apostle Paul gives us guidance in Philippians 4:8: "Finally, brethren, whatsoever things are true, whatsoever things are honorable, whatsoever things are just, whatsoever things are pure, whatsoever things are lovely, whatsoever things are of good report; if there be any virtue, and if there be any praise, think on these things" (ASV).

Where can we find such uplifting things, things that are good and true and pure? Look no further than the Word of God itself! Second Timothy 3:16-17 tells us that "all Scripture is given by inspiration of God, and is profitable for doctrine, for reproof, for correction, for instruction in righteousness, that the man of God may be complete, thoroughly equipped for every good work."

And if we have a personal relationship with Jesus Christ, then glory, grace, and truth accompany His presence: "And the Word became flesh and dwelt among us, and we beheld His glory, the glory as of the only begotten of the Father, full of grace and truth" (John 1:14).

So it is not only a matter of shunning the things of the world in order to counteract those forces, we also need to actively seek out and search God's Word.

If we have a personal relationship with Jesus Christ, then glory, grace, and truth accompany His presence.

How can I develop a deeper prayer life as I face the distractions of the world today?

One of the simplest responses to that question is found in Psalm 46. It begins with the recognition that "God is our refuge and strength, a very present help in trouble" (verse 1). We have God as our shelter, and His strength is available to help us when we pray! Later on in that Psalm we are reminded in verse 7 that "the Lord of hosts is with us; the God of Jacob is our refuge." What a wonderful thought that we are not alone when facing the distractions and problems of the world—God is with us! Then in verse 10 we are given the counsel to "be still, and know that I am God."

So as you go to God in prayer, the first step is to recognize where your strength comes from—for He is all powerful (omnipotent). Then acknowledge His presence—for He is always present (omnipresent). And finally, be quiet and still as you wait before Him—for He is all knowing (omniscient).

Prayer is a time of calming and quieting your soul before the Lord (Psalm 131:2). It is a precious opportunity to meet with the One who can provide the strength you need. Before you pray, recognize who He is and thank Him for answering your prayers according to His will and purpose. As you pray, commit your way to the Lord, trusting that God has heard your prayers, and He will bring it to pass (Psalm 37:5).

We are not alone when facing the distractions and problems of the world—God is with us!

What steps can I take to overcome my sin?

Only sin that is acknowledged can be overcome, so start by repenting of your sin. *Repentance* is the activity of reviewing one's actions and feeling contrition or regret for past wrongs, which is accompanied by commitment to change for the better. It means to change your mind; to turn and go the opposite way; to stop sinning. Next, confess your sin to God and to anyone you have sinned against and ask their forgiveness. Forgiveness brings freedom, and God grants forgiveness through the blood of Jesus (1 John 1:9). God will forgive you, and most people will forgive you too, if you ask them.

Then you need to make reparations where you can. If your actions have caused loss to others, you must restore what they have lost to the best of your ability. And finally, you must covenant with God to seek His power and to avoid repeating the sin. Regardless of how often you sin, you must resolve not to sin again (Job 31:1). Pray for God to give you the strength to resist temptation and refocus your mind on what is true and on the One who assures victory. Don't allow the guilt associated with your sin to keep you from asking God to forgive you and from finding the peace that only He can give!

Only sin that is acknowledged can be overcome.

Where can I find the strength to live a godly life?

As a believer, you have the strength of God in you waiting to be made manifest in your life. God stands ready, through the Holy Spirit, to grant you His strength. You must seek His strength, but He gives it to all who ask (1 Chronicles 29:12). For it is the Holy Spirit who strengthens and empowers you to live a godly life. He is the "muscle" waiting to be flexed and exercised and employed moment by moment in your life.

The Holy Spirit empowers you to love the Lord with all your heart, soul, mind, and strength (Mark 12:30). Therefore, you should love God with your mind by thinking on what is true, noble, just, pure, lovely, good, and praiseworthy (Philippians 4:8). You should love God with your soul by being committed to what He has established (Psalm 119:167).

And you should love God with your heart by keeping it pure, free from sin (1 Timothy 1:5). As you love God with all your heart, soul, and mind, you will love Him with all your strength, which is His strength—the strength needed to live a godly life.

> *Both riches and honor come from You, and You reign over all. In Your hand is power and might; in Your hand it is to make great and to give strength to all.*
>
> **1 CHRONICLES 29:12**

How can I live confidently as a Christian?

Developing confidence in your walk with God is built on four pillars:

1. **Knowing God's Word.**

   The Bible is full of "great and precious promises," and if you are a Christian, you are a partaker of the divine nature of God (2 Peter 1:4). Your confidence will develop as you know and meditate on the Word of God.

2. **Knowing your Heavenly Father.**

   Jesus said, "And this is eternal life, that they may know You, the only true God, and Jesus Christ whom You have sent" (John 17:3). You will gain confidence as your relationship with the Father deepens. Nothing should keep you from growing in your knowledge of Him.

3. **Investing your time, talent, and treasure in pursuing the Kingdom of God.**

   The apostle Paul lived confidently as he "press[ed] on .... Toward the goal for the prize of the upward call of God in Christ Jesus" (Philippians 3:12, 14). You can live confidently also as you pursue eternal investments in the Kingdom of God.

4. **Displaying confidence in your salvation through your witness to others.**

   The more you hear yourself sharing Christ, praising Christ, praying to Christ ... the more you'll realize you are living confidently for Christ.

What will help me persevere during difficult times?

Being prepared for difficult times helps you persevere when they come. Scripture tells us that trials are not uncommon and are a normal part of the Christian life (James 1:2). Paul reminded Timothy, "You … must endure hardship as a good soldier of Jesus Christ" (2 Timothy 2:3).

Finding balance in your Christian life equips you to endure. You must know the Word, be accountable to others, spend time in praise and worship, have a ministry of service, be memorizing Scripture—all are important. If you become weak in one area, other strengths will help you persevere.

Forging bonds with people who keep up their spirits and stay faithful in kingdom work even during dark days encourages you to endure. If you stumble and fall along the way, nothing will get you on your feet faster than the extended hand of a strong friend.

Focusing on Christ and what He's done for you will keep you moving forward. As you keep your eyes on Him, you will run with endurance (Hebrews 12:2).

> *My brethren, count it all joy when you fall into various trials, knowing that the testing of your faith produces patience. But let patience have its perfect work, that you may be perfect and complete, lacking nothing.*
>
> **JAMES 1:2-4**

What are the benefits to remaining "cool under fire"?

Scripture teaches us that God uses ordinary people in very stressful situations and environments and empowers them to stay "cool under fire." Think of Esther in her valiant approach into the inner court of the king without an invitation. God was with her and the king extended his scepter to her, saving her from a sentence of death.

The first benefit to remaining composed and controlled during a stressful situation or trial is seeing how God is changing you into the image of Christ. As God's grace is at work in your life, you learn to trust God more and more in every situation. Think of how you responded to stress, trials, and trouble before you met Christ; now think of how you respond to those same things today. The growth you made is an encouragement that God is indeed working in your life.

The second benefit to remaining "cool under fire" is testifying to others that the power of God can change their lives too. Jesus' disciples were transformed by being around Him and watching the power of God in His life. After Jesus returned to heaven, the apostles boldly impacted the Jewish leaders and the people of Jerusalem. In the same way, your confidence and faith in God can influence others to trust in Him.

Let your light so shine before men, that they may see your good works and glorify your Father in heaven.

MATTHEW 5:16

How can I determine God's will for me?

The Word of God contains the will of God; and in all the major areas of thought, speech, and conduct the will of God is clear. For example, 1 Thessalonians 4:3 says, "For this is the will of God, your sanctification: that you should abstain from sexual immorality." Peter says to respect authority, "for this is the will of God" (1 Peter 2:15). And 1 Thessalonians 5:16-18 says, "Rejoice always, pray without ceasing, in everything give thanks; for this is the will of God in Christ Jesus for you."

These basic commands will help you learn God's will and understand His direction for your life as you grow in the grace and maturity needed for the times we live in. God's will for your life is demonstrated by following His commands in Scripture—letting your good works be evidence of your faith

(Matthew 5:16), putting no limit on the extent of your forgiveness (Matthew 18:21-22), and guarding against the flesh (Matthew 26:41).

You will be doing God's will as you obey His commands.

What should I do to keep my mind under God's control?

Keeping your mind under God's control starts with receiving the truth of the Gospel. All the treasures of wisdom and knowledge dwell in Christ, and when you receive Him, God replaces your spirit of fear with power, love, and a sound mind (2 Timothy 1:7). Next, you need to fill your mind with God's Word. Every temptation comes to you through your thoughts; therefore, you must evaluate what you read, see, study, and hear. You must let the Word of Christ dwell in you richly (Colossians 3:16). Finally, you are to meditate on Scripture day and night. Biblical meditation is the powerful practice of pondering, personalizing, and practicing Scripture.

Romans 8:5 says, "For those who live according to the flesh set their minds on the things of the flesh, but those who live according to the Spirit, the things of the Spirit." God's Word should be constantly circulating through your mind so that you begin seeing things as He does. Through this your mind is renewed and kept under God's control.

> *God's Word should be constantly circulating through your mind so that you begin seeing things as He does.*

How does our speech represent Christ to the world?

Sometimes we open our mouths and we wonder, "Where did that come from?" The goal of Christians should be for our speech to be characterized by the values found in Scripture. Proverbs 10:19 says, "In the multitude of words sin is not lacking, but he who restrains his lips is wise." Sometimes the best thing we can do is to show restraint and hold our tongue—even when we are challenged or treated unfairly. It can be hurtful and even harmful to say the first thing that comes to our mind; it is much better to measure our words with restraint.

The Bible tells us to use a measure of wisdom when we speak. Luke 6:45 says, "For out of the abundance of the heart [the] mouth speaks." Wise words flow from wise hearts, and wise hearts thrive on a daily diet of Scripture and prayer. Words spoken with a measure of wisdom leave a testimony that accomplishes much for Christ. Whenever we have the occasion to share our faith, it should be done with a measure of grace. "Let your speech always be with grace, seasoned with salt, that you may know how you ought to answer each one" (Colossians 4:6). As we learn to guard our speech with wisdom, our ability to show Christ and His grace to the world will expand.

Wise words flow from wise hearts, and wise hearts thrive on a daily diet of Scripture and prayer.

How am I to treat those around me who are hurting?

As a Christian, the key to showing God's love is to have compassion on those around you. *Compassion* means "to suffer with," and showing compassion is about using what you have—money, talent, encouragement, or a shoulder to cry on—to meet another person's need. When Jesus told the story of the Good Samaritan in Luke 10, it was compassion that caused the Samaritan to stop and help the man who lay injured by the side of the road. He accepted the inconvenience of going to the other side of the road where the Priest and the Levite walked past previously. He showed practical, godly love in action as he cared for the man, putting him on his own donkey, taking him to an inn, and providing for his care for an extended period. He put goodness and mercy into action.

The compassion Jesus demonstrated to others while He was on earth is to be continued through you as well (Matthew 15:32; Mark 6:34; Luke 7:13). God intends for you to see the needs of others and respond to those needs. First Peter 3:8 says, "Be of one mind, having compassion for one another." Paul told the Ephesians to "be patient, bearing with one another in love" and "be kind and compassionate to one another" (Ephesians 4:2, 32, NIV). Those around you will know the compassion of Christ by your demonstration of it to them.

> *God intends for you to see the needs of others and respond to those needs.*

How can I encourage other followers of Christ?

The Lord wants to make you a walking, breathing dispenser of divine encouragement to other Christians. Hebrews 10:25, NIV, says you're to encourage others "all the more" as the day of Christ's return draws closer. There's tremendous comfort in meditating on the Lord's return, contemplating the Resurrection and Rapture, and thinking of your heavenly home. In 1 Thessalonians 4, the apostle Paul reminded believers that the Lord was coming suddenly, with a shout, with the voice of an archangel, with the trumpet call of God. The dead in Christ would rise first. Those Christians who were alive and remained would be snatched up in the air to forever be with the Lord. First Thessalonians 4:18 says, "Therefore comfort one another with these words." In that verse, the Bible gives you a mandate to encourage others with the reality of Christ's coming. If the return of Christ is a clear and present awareness in your mind, it will spill over into your conversation, and whenever you speak of His coming, others will be comforted and encouraged.

Then we who are alive and remain shall be caught up together with them in the clouds to meet the Lord in the air. And thus we shall always be with the Lord. Therefore comfort one another with these words.
1 THESSALONIANS 4:17-18

What can I do to display Christ to those around me?

Your appearance and actions are simply extensions of your thoughts and values. Others can tell a great deal about you by the language you use, the habits you keep, the friends you make, and the places you frequent. As you honor God in these areas of life, those you interact with regularly will see Christ in you. And those who don't know you should recognize a difference in you by your compassion, friendliness, benevolence, generosity, and acts of kindness. Displaying Christ may be as simple as smiling at a store clerk and engaging with them in friendly conversation. It might mean visiting a local nursing home and chatting with the elderly or praying with the lonely.

This world is starved for love, joy, peace, patience, kindness, faithfulness, radiance, simplicity, honesty, and compassion. As a Christian, make it your purpose to specialize in those characteristics. As your actions reflect these attributes, the light of Christ will be shown as you "let your light so shine before men, that they may see your good works and glorify [our] Father" (Matthew 5:16).

This world is starved for love, joy, peace, patience, kindness, faithfulness, radiance, simplicity, honesty, and compassion.

How can I be an influencer in today's world?

Influence is the outcome of a life that is dedicated to serving the Lord. Just as Christ was a servant, we need to have a servant's heart as well. As we make God and serving others through Him a priority in our life, everything else will fall into proper order.

As you develop a worshipful attitude, you'll find it more natural to witness to others.

Out of your love for God, you will develop a heart for worship. Worship is a daily attitude of loving God, singing His praises, trusting His promises, thanking Him for the little joys, pondering His creative genius, and telling Him you love Him. As you develop a worshipful attitude, you'll become more sensitive to the promptings of the Holy Spirit and find it more natural to witness to others. The Holy Spirit will prompt you to share the Gospel with a friend or a stranger. Your worship and witness will be reflected in your daily work for Christ. Psalm 112 says, "How joyful are those who fear the Lord and delight in obeying His commands .... They are generous, compassionate, and righteous .... Their good deeds will be remembered forever. They will have influence and honor" (verses 1, 4, 9, NLT). As you worship, witness, and work for the Lord, your life will influence the world around you for Christ.

How can I maintain a calm spirit in times of trouble?

In order to maintain a calm spirit in times of trouble, preparation begins with your mind. To begin the process, gather some scriptural promises you can claim. You should expect attacks from the enemy and the challenge of trials in life, so you need to store up Scriptures to shield your mind and heart. Proverbs 10:14 says, "Wise people store up knowledge." Read, study, learn, memorize, and meditate on God's Word day and night. The Lord will give you verses to store away for times of difficulty. Next, collect scriptural blessings you can count. Follow David's example from the book of Psalms and count your blessings in the midst of trouble. Learn to find something good in every situation and thank God for it. Be sure to end each day by thanking God for His goodness to you. Then, collect scriptural attitudes to claim for your life. The Bible teaches that our faith, trust, and confidence comes from Him, and that we have nothing to fear with Him on our side (Psalm 27). Remember, you have instant access to the throne of grace, and your God is a very present help in times of trouble—a mighty fortress!

> *The Lord is my light and my salvation; whom shall I fear? The Lord is the strength of my life; of whom shall I be afraid?*
>
> **PSALM 27:1**

Company

Therefore, beloved, looking forward
to these things, be diligent to be
found by Him in peace, without
spot and blameless.

2 PETER 3:14

How can I develop wise, godly friendships?

The art of selecting the right friends is one of life's greatest skills. Start by asking yourself if you are stronger or weaker in your faith after spending time with your friends. Your closest friends, the ones who influence you the most, should build you up rather than pull you down. To develop these types of friendships, imitate the Lord Jesus and take the initiative in loving others. Identify needs in the lives of those around you and quietly seek to meet those needs. Look for the lonely and love them. Ask God to give you a handful of people for whom to pray. Be there in difficult times. Laugh with those who laugh and weep with those who weep. Be a friend, build good friendships, and then keep those friendships in good repair. As you reach out to others in friendship, you will develop a group of wise, godly friends who will help you grow in your faith.

*He who walks
with wise men will
be wise, but the
companion of fools
will be destroyed.*

PROVERBS 13:20

> *The things that you have heard from me among many witnesses, commit these to faithful men who will be able to teach others also.*

2 TIMOTHY 2:2

How can I leave a godly legacy for my family and friends?

The heart of a godly legacy is love. Love for God is the legacy and the method for passing on that legacy. Love is both the means and the end. One of the first ways to leave a godly legacy is by reading God's Word. Others should observe you regularly reading Scripture and see it transforming your life. You should also be a person of prayer—consistently praying for the needs of family and friends. It's important to live an honest life, for those closest to you are quick to pick up on personal inconsistencies. Finally, leave an enduring testimony. Wherever you are in the legacy chain of passing on the love of God to your children and grandchildren, continue walking in the love of Christ.

Remember: Spend time in His Word. Pray for others. Live above reproach. Teach others what you've learned.

As a Christian, how can I reach others with the Gospel?

No matter where you live or where you've been, you have a mission—to take the Good News of Christ to the ends of the earth and to bring the Gospel within earshot of anyone willing to listen. The process originates when you ask God to give you a burden for the lost and you begin praying for them. Make a list of family, friends, and others in your sphere of influence who need Christ. As you pray, a sense of expectancy will fill your soul for the lost. God will answer in His own timing and way, and He will use you in the process.

Next, pray for open doors to share the Gospel. Actively look for opportunities to share the Gospel and pray for wisdom as you interact with others. You never know when a word of witness or a simple verse of Scripture will lodge in someone's heart and lead to more conversations about the Gospel.

When doors open, share the Good News.

What is the best way for me to invest my resources in the times we live in?

Knowing how to invest your resources in the times we live in begins with knowing God's heart and spending time growing in an awareness of His priorities, values, and plans. Jesus served others during His time here on earth, and you should faithfully use your resources to benefit those whom Jesus came to serve. Jesus came into the world for an eternal purpose—to free those held captive by Satan so they might be restored to a life of fellowship with their Creator for all eternity. As His faithful steward, eternal redemption must be the foundation of your concern for others at any time, but especially today.

Jesus chose to invest Himself in meeting the needs of others when He came to earth—He met their spiritual, physical, and eternal requirements. He sacrificially did this through

His life and death. He met the physical and spiritual needs of people, and you are called to do the same. As you follow Christ and the leading of the Holy Spirit, you will find causes in which to invest your time, talent, and treasure—ones in which service and sacrifice produce both temporal and eternal results.

> *Eternal redemption must be the foundation of your concern for others at any time.*

What are some ways I can express love and gratitude to those around me?

It's easy to take family and friends for granted, yet they are the ones to whom your demonstrations of love should most often be directed. Spend some time in prayer and consider how you can express your love and gratitude to these people in a unique way. Here are just a few ways you can demonstrate love and thankfulness to your family and friends.

- Write notes to your spouse and/or children and place them around your home.

- Set aside time for a special family meal and tell each person how much you love them.

- Bake a special dessert and take it to work to share with your coworkers.

- Call a close friend just to see how they are doing and see if they have any needs that they would like you to pray about.

- Send a care package to family member or friend who is away at college or in the military—including the message that they are in your prayers.

- Surprise your children with an unexpected after-school treat.

- Serve your spouse by completing one of their normal duties around your home.

As you begin to demonstrate love and thankfulness for others, you will be blessed in return. The world we live in has become a place of emojis and quick texts, so anything you can do to express your love through an action or deed will be an encouragement to those around you and exemplify Christ's devotion through your loving service.

> **How can I live an authentic life for Christ and be a witness to those around me?**

People are watching how you live, what you say, and what you do. And to be an authentic witness, you must first be authentic in your commitment to Christ. Christ must be first, last, and always in your life. He must be the Lord and Master of your life. When you're authentic in your commitment, you'll live out that commitment in your conduct. You'll treat others with gracious humility, and you'll be known for your integrity and honesty. As a child of God, you should be increasingly growing into the image of Christ and reflecting Him to a lost world—that is the process of sanctification. It leads to being compassionate and full of good works like our Lord. "And above all things have fervent love for one another, for 'love will cover a multitude of sins.' Be hospitable to one another without grumbling. As each one has received a gift, minister it to one another as good stewards of the manifold grace of God" (1 Peter 4:8-10). Your love for others, as demonstrated through your servanthood, will be the most authentic representation of Christ, and bear witness for Christ, to the world around you.

Christ must be first, last, and always in your life.

Therefore submit to God. Resist the devil and he will flee from you. Draw near to God and He will draw near to you. Cleanse your hands, you sinners; and purify your hearts, you double-minded. Lament and mourn and weep! Let your laughter be turned to mourning and your joy to gloom. Humble yourselves in the sight of the Lord, and He will lift you up. Do not speak evil of one another, brethren. He who speaks evil of a brother and judges his brother, speaks evil of the law and judges the law. But if you judge the law, you are not a doer of the law but a judge.

JAMES 4:7-11

What are some principles for showing grace to other Christians?

In James 4:7-11, there are nine principles that will help you show grace to fellow believers.

1. *Relinquish control of your life.*
   Verse 7 says, "Therefore submit to God." You must willingly yield control of your life to God.

2. *Resist the devil.*
   The second half of verse 7 states: "Resist the devil and he will flee from you." To do this, you are to implement the armor of God (Ephesians 6:10-18), saturate yourself with God's Word (Matthew 4:4), and pray (1 John 5:14-15).

3. *Restore worship to a priority.*
   "Draw near to God and He will draw near to you" (verse 8).

4. *Renounce sinful actions.*

In verse 8, James says, "Cleanse your hands, you sinners." You should let go of any actions which are a violation of God's holy standards and righteousness.

5. *Reject sinful attitudes.*

James continues, "And purify your hearts, you double-minded" (verse 8). You cannot love God and love the world at the same time.

6. *React to sin with sorrow.*

You are to "lament and mourn and weep" over the sin in your life (verse 9).

7. *Refrain from a frivolous attitude toward evil.*

"Let your laughter be turned to mourning and your joy to gloom" (verse 9). When you comprehend the severity of sin, you will be saddened by it.

8. *Respond humbly to success.*

Verse 10 says, "Humble yourselves in the sight of the Lord, and He will lift you up."

9. *Refuse to slander your brother.*

You should not speak evil about other Christians. James clearly states: "Do not speak evil of one another, brethren" (verse 11).

As you focus your heart and your attitude toward rejecting sin in your life, you will become more aware of God's grace to you, demonstrating His grace to other Christians in return.

> *Draw near to God and He will draw near to you.*
> **JAMES 4:8**

How can I be used by God in the world I live in today?

The Christian in today's world needs to impart the fragrance of Christ. "For we are to God the fragrance of Christ among those who are being saved and among those who are perishing" (2 Corinthians 2:15). Begin by being a refreshing person—someone who boosts the spirit of others and imparts energy and courage to them. Your words and actions can give encouragement to fellow Christians as they seek to live for Christ. Philemon is an example of this: "For we have great joy and consolation in your love, because the hearts of the saints have been refreshed by you, brother" (Philemon 7). Continue by remembering other believers in prayer. Faithfully pray for other Christians and let them know you are praying for them. In addition to encouraging fellow believers with your words and praying for them, be good to them.

Galatians 6:10 says, "Therefore, as we have opportunity, let us do good to all, especially to those who are of the household of faith." Finally, labor together with others for the sake of the Gospel. In 1 Corinthians 3:9, Paul says that all Christians are God's fellow workers together. And there is no camaraderie like that which is built among those who labor in ministry together.

Your words and actions can give encouragement to fellow Christians as they seek to live for Christ.

How can I be a true friend?

Sometimes our friends have problems and challenges in their lives that are unique to them, and it's not always easy to identify with what they are experiencing, but we can become a true friend as we embody the following traits:

- A true friend is dauntless; they aren't afraid to walk with their companions through the dark valleys of life.

- A true friend is also committed. If friendship is worth anything at all, it is worth committing to—going the extra mile, paying the extra price, giving of your time and energy, and demonstrating extra zeal.

- Finally, a true or real friend is consistent. They aren't just a friend on occasion; they show up day after day and year after year.

Jesus is a true friend. His love for us is consistent. He endured scorn and rejection on earth—He is dauntless—so that we might be with Him in heaven one day. Jesus is a heroic committed friend to all who have entered into a faith relationship with Him. He is the friend who "sticks closer than a brother" (Proverbs 18:24). And you can be this type of friend too—by walking alongside your friends when they are experiencing trials, by going the extra mile to care for them in their need, and by consistently loving them without condemnation.

He is the friend who "sticks closer than a brother."

How can I live selflessly as part of the Body of Christ?

Living selflessly as part of the Body of Christ begins with being willing to play a supporting role and empowering others in their spiritual walk. Each of us is called to be involved in evangelism by sharing the Gospel and by contributing to those who are proclaiming the Truth to the lost. By giving to the mission outreach of the Gospel, you are helping to provide a financial base for the Gospel to go forward in a multitude of ways.

Additionally, each Christian is given spiritual gifts to edify the Body of Christ. Part of living selflessly as a part of the Body of Christ is contributing in the way God has gifted you to minister. Every time you selflessly serve in the opportunities God puts before you, you are contributing to a larger picture that will bear fruit over time. Your efforts, combined with the efforts of other selfless believers, move the Church forward in extending the Gospel to your community and the world. By selflessly supporting and encouraging the work of God in every way you can, you are participating in the ministry of the Body of Christ.

There are differences of ministries, but the same Lord. And there are diversities of activities, but it is the same God who works all in all.

1 CORINTHIANS 12:5-6

Commitment

Let your heart therefore be loyal to the
Lord our God, to walk in His statutes
and keep His commandments.

1 KINGS 8:61

I want Jesus to be more than a symbol in my life; I want Him to be my Lord and Savior. What is the first step I should take?

Sadly, to many people, Jesus, the Church, and Christianity are societal trappings of our culture instead of life-changing realities. They don't realize that it is vital to know Him personally. He isn't a "dashboard Jesus," a symbol that you place somewhere in your car or in your life. He isn't plastic; He's powerful. He's not small; He's infinite. He's not a good-luck token; He's the risen and reigning Lord of time and eternity.

Perhaps there's no Savior in your life. Perhaps you've never turned your life over to the real Jesus of history and Scripture. There is a Creator-God who made us and gave us eternal souls, but something went wrong in our heart. Our imperfections and iniquities have alienated us from His glory. That's why He became a man—the God-Man, Christ Jesus—and came to earth and died on Calvary's cross for our sins. He rose from the grave on the third day, and He offers us eternal life for the taking. The Bible says, "If you confess with your mouth the Lord Jesus and believe in your heart that God has raised Him from the dead, you will be saved" (Romans 10:9).

You can bow your head right now—wherever you are … in your home, at a coffee shop, on an airplane, in a hospital room, or in your car, staring at the dashboard—and quietly ask the Lord Jesus to forgive your sins, redeem your life, and become your Savior. He's waiting now to enter your heart. Why don't you let Him come in?

He's the risen and reigning Lord
of time and eternity.

What are some ways that I can develop and keep an active faith?

The book of Hebrews tells us that without faith it is impossible to please God (11:6). Yet how many of us can define faith and how it has worked in our life? The anatomy of faith remains a mystery to many Christians. Faith isn't just a biblical term to study. It's a dynamic principle of living. And if we experience it regularly, we will find ourselves in the best spiritual shape of our life.

What is involved in exercising your faith? I've defined the anatomy of an active faith with the help of some familiar exercises.

SIT-UPS

Sit under the teaching of the Word of God every week. The Greek word for church, *ecclesia*, is found more than one hundred times in the

New Testament, underscoring the importance of the Church. It's alarming to me how many Christians today have allowed their minds to be filled with the garbage of this world. What you put into your mind programs your life. That's why it so important to hear God's Word on a continual basis.

100-YARD DASH

Be ready to run to the aid of a hurting soul and demonstrate God's love. We were not created to live and function alone. We need one another for help and support. Ecclesiastes 4:9-10 says that "Two are better than one .... For if they fall, one will lift up his companion."

PUSH-UPS

Be an encourager. In the same way a traditional push-up strengthens your chest and shoulder muscles, lifting up a person in need builds your spiritual muscles. Second Corinthians 1:4

speaks of the Father of mercies "who comforts us in all our tribulation, that we may be able to comfort those who are in any trouble, with the comfort with which we ourselves are comforted by God." Christians who have been encouraged by God should be the world's best at encouraging others.

DEEP KNEE BENDS

Pray daily. If we want the Lord's blessing on our life, there is no substitute for the prescription of prayer. The apostle Paul urges us in Colossians 4:2 to "continue earnestly in prayer, being vigilant in it." It takes effort and commitment to confess your sins before God and to pray for guidance for yourself and others. Prayer is perhaps one of the most difficult disciplines to practice as a Christian, but it leads to spiritual fitness and vitality.

LUNGES

Lunge into Christian service. Some of us avoid ministry altogether. When God shows you a need that you can fill, get involved and see the Holy Spirit work through you. First Corinthians 12:7 says, "But the manifestation of the Spirit is given to each one for the profit of all."

STRETCHING

Ask God to stretch you beyond your comfort zone. When I was in seventh grade, my father left his pastorate at a prosperous church to become the president of a struggling Baptist college of less than ninety students. Many people told him he was throwing his career away, but in reality He was stretching his faith. I learned as I watched my father that faith is a life-changing truth. Is God asking you to stretch out in faith in a specific area of your life?

WALKING

Walk in the Word daily. Matthew 4:4 says, "Man shall not live by bread alone, but by every word that proceeds from the mouth of God." Reading the Bible is like exercise. Some days you don't feel like doing it, but you know it's good for you. You can't have a growing, flourishing life unless the Word of God is at the core of your being. Discipline yourself for godliness by making it a habit to read the Bible every day.

JUMPING HURDLES

Share your faith—no matter what the obstacle! Jesus' last words in the Great Commission, "Go therefore and make disciples of all the nations" (Matthew 28:19), make it clear that we should be passionate about sharing the Gospel. Witnessing can seem as impossible as jumping over a tall hurdle! An active faith enables us to overcome the obstacles of fear, apathy, and pride in order to say, "Lord, I'm willing to share your love with anyone You place in my life."

Are you routinely practicing these eight exercises for an active faith? Being consistent is key because a "stop-start" exercise regimen rarely produces lasting results.

If you want to make a new start in your spiritual fitness routine, consult your physician—the Great Physician, Jesus Christ. Ask God to help you practice daily spiritual disciplines that will increase your faith.

> **When I don't understand the circumstances of my life or the world today, how can I discover God's sovereign plan for me?**

When we look at our world today, we're apt to ask: Who's in charge? Wars raging. Morality collapsing. Infections spreading. Hearts failing. Children suffering. The Bible declares, "The Lord is in control .... Yours is the mighty power and glory and victory and majesty. Everything in the heavens and earth is yours, O Lord .... We adore you as being in control of everything" (1 Kings 20:13, CEV; 1 Chronicles 29:11, TLB).

While Bible-taught believers know that God is sovereign, sometimes the message doesn't get from our head to our heart. One thing is certain: The God who is in control is infinitely elevated above His creatures. He is the Lord of heaven and earth. He is subject to none.

He is influenced by none. He is absolutely independent, free, and in control. No one can hinder Him, compel Him, or stop Him. He is in control. Psalm 103:19 says, "The Lord has established His throne in heaven, and His kingdom rules over all."

God has a plan for the nations and it is the unfolding of His plan as the world moves inexorably towards its preordained end. Dr. A. T. Pierson, put it well: "Prophecy and Providence are...twin sisters.... Back of all these apparently capricious, conflicting and accidental changes of human history, there is an infinite God, whose omniscience and omnipresence forbid that anything should escape his knowledge or evade his power, and whose goodness assures a benevolent design, even behind seeming disaster."

This means we shouldn't panic during times of national and international uncertainty. It's easy to watch the news every night at bedtime, then retire depressed and discouraged. How much better to turn off the television and open the Bible at bedtime, then go to sleep reassured that "The Lord is great, and our Lord is above all gods. Whatever the Lord pleases He does, in heaven and in earth" (Psalm 135:5-6).

One of the most comforting truths in the Bible is that the sovereign providence of God extends to the daily details of our life. He isn't just concerned about the nations, but about the sparrows, the lilies—and you. His control extends over all our days and all our ways, and He is able to work all things together for our good. So when you read frightening headlines…when you face adversity in life and disappointment slaps you across the face…when your world seems to be coming apart and you aren't sure what's going on, remember—God is Sovereign. He is in control. He works all things for His glory and for our good.

> **How can I ensure that my faith is growing deeper and stronger?**

Consistency is found throughout God's economy—the turning of the seasons, the movement of heavenly bodies, the replication of the genetic code throughout generations. In everything, God seems to say, "Be consistent." God Himself is life's greatest example of consistency: "For I am the Lord, I do not change" (Malachi 3:6).

If everything in God's creation grows consistently, little by little, how might we expect to grow spiritually as reborn followers of Christ? That's right—consistently, little by little. Follow me on this line of thought: The key to spiritual growth is not Bible study or prayer or giving or service or worship. The key to spiritual growth is engaging in *all* those disciplines *consistently*.

We grow spiritually like an old-time miner who searched for gold or silver on his own. With a pick and shovel, he dug his hole and picked at the rocks—daily, consistently, expectantly until he reached his goal. That's exactly the image Solomon gives us in Proverbs 2:4: We should be working toward growth like we are looking "for hidden treasures." That kind of growth takes patience and consistency. Not too fast, not too slow, but just the right progress day by day.

Remember that God is infinite. His wisdom is limitless; we don't grow up in Christ in a day. His ways are deep and wonderful, and it takes years of prayerful experience to search them out. Every day should be an adventure as you discover more about Him and grow in your faith.

> **Why is the hope for the world found only in the Gospel of Jesus Christ?**

In the diversity of cultures around the world, there are many religions that try to offer hope, but they fail every time. They only offer conditional rescue in gods of their making. But Jesus said, "Come to Me, all you who labor and are heavy laden," and "If anyone thirsts, let him come to Me and drink," and these words of comfort and hope: "God did not send His Son into the world to condemn the world, but that the world through Him might be saved" (Matthew 11:28; John 7:37; John 3:17). What do those who come to Jesus find that they cannot find in any other other religion in the world?

- Salvation without deeds: Christ is the "end of the law" for all who believe (Romans 10:4).

- Salvation without difficulty: It is as near as one's own heart and mouth (Romans 10:8).

- Salvation without deception: Confession is the evidence of belief; you can know you're saved (Romans 10:9).

- Salvation without disappointment: "You will be saved" (Romans 10:9).

- Salvation without distinction: Anyone can be saved (Romans 10:13).

- Salvation without discrimination: No ethnic or racial group is excluded from the Gospel (Romans 10:12).

Why is it possible for the Christian Gospel to offer such hope? Because it offers what no human being can ever attain: a righteous standing before a holy God. Because He was the God-Man, Jesus Christ was the only sinless human being who ever lived. He died a sinner's death in our place and offers us His righteousness in exchange for believing in Him.

No other religion in the world offers so much in exchange for faith—for accepting the gift of salvation God offers in Christ. No wonder so many adherents of other religions, once they understand the simplicity of the Christian Gospel, embrace Jesus with open arms—He is the hope of the world.

> **My walk with God seems to be at a standstill. What are the next steps I should take to draw closer to Him?**

First, cultivate a sense of wonder. When was the last time you noticed the rose blooming by the fence? The spangled sky on a clear and moonless night? When was the last time you stood amazed in the presence of Jesus the Nazarene?

There's more to Christianity than you and I have thus far experienced; there's more to God than we've learned; there's more to the Bible than we've discovered so far.

Remember when you first met God and experienced His amazing grace? Wasn't that a wonderful discovery? But how long has it been since you glimpsed something new in your relationship with Him? Have you lost the wonder? Cultivate your curiosity, and stay fresh. Look for new discoveries every day, and enjoy His mercies which are new every morning.

Second, ask God to show you previously undiscovered truths in the Bible, like the psalmist who prayed, "Open my eyes, that I may see wondrous things from Your law" (Psalm 119:18).

Sometimes when we read a familiar passage of Scripture, we pass over it quickly, assuming we've already seen and studied it. But could there be more insights still waiting to be uncovered?

The Bible is simple enough for a child to understand, but deep enough to occupy a brilliant scholar for a dozen lifetimes. Its meaning doesn't change, but our understanding of its message and its application to our life is a process of daily discovery that rivals any exploration in history. Someone once said that Bible students are "wide-eyed travelers in the midst of wonders." Have you learned something new in the Bible this week?

Now to Him who is able to do exceedingly abundantly above all that we ask or think, according to the power that works in us.

EPHESIANS 3:20

What is the first step toward trusting God with every aspect of my life?

The ironic reality is that people will often trust big, man-made machines with their very lives—planes, trains, and automobiles—but have a hard time trusting a God who is infinitely bigger and stronger than all of them put together. Here's the problem with that kind of thinking: *The size of the object of your faith determines the size of the outcome of your faith.* You need to see God in all His infinite glory, and power, in order to trust Almighty God with your life now and for all eternity.

If you have a small God, you are walking by sight rather than by faith. Small-God thinkers already know the answer to what they're praying for, or they're praying for something so inconsequential that the outcome is irrelevant. But big-God thinkers walk and think biblically—by faith. They pursue dreams and opportunities so big that they are beyond anything man could pull off; so big that, unless God does it, their dream is doomed to failure.

Remember when Moses went before Pharaoh with nothing but a wooden staff and told him to let his kinsmen go? That was big-God thinking. If God didn't provide, the people were doomed to slavery, and Moses was doomed to die.

Remember when Daniel and his three friends were thrown into a den of lions and a fiery furnace respectively because they wouldn't submit to a pagan king? That was big-God thinking. If God didn't save them, they'd have died in Babylon.

Remember when Joshua was told to bring down Jericho with trumpets instead of swords? When Gideon was told to defeat the Midianites with jars and torches? When Elijah asked God to set soggy wood on fire to defeat the prophets of Baal? They were all big-God thinkers too. They attempted something so big it was doomed to fail unless God showed up.

Remember when Jesus willingly let Himself be put to death because He believed that in less than 48 hours, God would give Him back His life and raise Him from the dead? That was big-God thinking. If Jesus could believe God for that need, we can believe God for our greatest need too.

The reason the apostle could write these words—"Now to Him who is able to do exceedingly abundantly above all that we ask or think, according to the power that works in us" (Ephesians 3:20)—is that he was a big-God thinker. Because Paul knew how big God is, he knew to expect great things. His expectations of God were based on his knowledge of God. Become a big-God thinker and walk by faith.

Does God have a mission for each of His children?

Even if you don't remember the television series, no doubt you would recognize the theme music for the more recent movies with the same title, *Mission: Impossible*. At the beginning of every episode on the television show, the team's leader received a mysterious recording explaining a crisis situation. And there would always be this challenge: "Your mission, should you choose to accept it, is …" Of course, the team always accepted the mission—and accomplished it.

God is saying the same to us: He sent His Son to earth on a mission to destroy the work of Satan (1 John 3:8). And He has chosen you to be His agents throughout the earth. You have been given all you need to fulfill this mission, but I must warn you—it is dangerous. Some have died, many have suffered, and all have been tested. But for those who accept this mission and fulfill it, there is great reward. I ask you now: "Will you become an agent of the Lord Jesus Christ and commit your life to the greater good of bringing many into the Kingdom of God?"

The message of the mission is always the same (Matthew 28:18-20), but the strategy changes, and the stakes grow higher each day as the return of Jesus Christ draws near. Just as the lead agent on *Mission: Impossible* was given a dossier of information to use in accomplishing his specific mission, we have one as well. In light of the day and time in which we live, our dossier is this: the prophetic portions of Scripture outlining the future of planet earth.

Have you studied this material? Are you clear about what the future holds, prophetically speaking? Can you sketch an overview timeline of God's prophetic timetable to share with a friend who doesn't know Christ—who knows nothing about biblical prophecy or how specific it is?

In today's world, most people are insecure, even fearful, about the future. Every Christian should be an "in-secret" agent-in-training, studying the prophetic portions of Scripture along with the Gospel. The mission is yours. Will you accept the mission and become God's prophetic agent in these tumultuous times?

> *He has chosen you to be His agents throughout the earth.*

In light of the world we live in today, should I have a personal mission statement of faith for my walk with God?

The answer is "Yes." Many famous people who had a great impact on our world crafted and followed a vision statement. Or, to use contemporary language, they created a mission statement.

Mission statements say who we are, what we believe, and what we want to accomplish. They become tracks to run on, roads to travel on, and destinations to reach.

God has a plan, a job, a calling for each of us to fulfill. The more intimately we walk with Christ, and the longer we serve Him, the better we will gain a sense of what our personal mission for Christ is. We don't need to invent it—we need to discover it. Pray and ask God for His wisdom. Take time to work through developing your mission statement of faith. And then, begin merging your life with your mission. A mission statement is not to hang on the wall or stick in your Bible. It is a benchmark you use to evaluate your life over time.

To create your own mission statement of faith, begin here:

1. Identify past successes. How has God used you in the past? Where do others think you've been fruitful?

2. Identify core values. Brainstorm the values and beliefs that most define who you are.

3. Identify contributions. What skills, resources, talents, and passions do you possess?

4. Identify goals. If you could do anything for the cause of Christ in this world, what would you do?

5. Write down your mission statement.

This exercise is about taking a fresh look at who you are. It means recognizing that no Christian in the world is like you. It means discovering the "good works" that God saved you by grace to walk in (Ephesians 2:8-10). It means believing that your days were written in God's Book before you were born (Psalm 139:16).

Today is the day to begin fulfilling your mission for God.

> **I know that God is the great Promise Keeper, but how can I claim His promises for my life?**

God makes the promises, but we have to claim them. From where we stand, a promise not claimed and acted upon has the same practical effect as a promise never made. If I promise to help you whenever you call me, but you never call, you never receive the benefit of my promise. God is the Promise Maker; but we are the promise claimers.

There is no list of "all the promises of God" in Scripture. Instead, we find them as we read from Genesis to Revelation and discover the character of God. Whether spoken explicitly or revealed implicitly, all of God's promises are rooted in His character. For instance, "I will never leave you nor forsake you" (Hebrews 13:5) is an explicit promise to all Christians. But God's promise directly to the apostle Paul—"My grace is sufficient for you, for My strength is made perfect in weakness" (2 Corinthians 12:9)—is also an implicit promise to all believers. Paul spoke for all of us when he said, "For when I am weak, then I am strong [in Christ]" (verse 10). God is no respecter of persons. If the power of Christ was available to Paul, it is likewise available to us by implication.

Therefore, our task is to know the character of God so well that we can take His very being and presence as a promise, a promise made incarnate in the Person of Jesus Christ. As far back as Abraham, the people of God have been seeking the same thing we seek: "a better, that is, a heavenly country. Therefore God is not ashamed to be called their God, for He has prepared a city for them" (Hebrews 11:16). And He has promised a better country and city for us as well. But in the interim, it is His promises about life on planet earth we need to embrace.

I love the six categories of God's promises outlined in *The Life Promises Bible* and commend them to you for your own meditation:

- Promises About God's Principles: God has spoken, and His words are true.

- Promises About God's Presence: God is with us now and forever.

- Promises About God's Provision: God's resources are unlimited and are ours.

- Promises About God's Protection: God's purposes are our shield.

- Promises About God's Plan: God's desires are settled in heaven.

- Promises About God's Preparation: God's goal is to spend eternity with us.[1]

What more do we need in this life than those six areas of promise?

---

[1] Kenneth Boa, general editor, *The Life Promises Bible — A One-Year Study of God's Presence, Provision, and Plan for You* (Grand Rapids: Zondervan Publishing House, 2001).

> **In the chaotic world we live in, how can I best share the peace that Jesus gives with people in my sphere of influence?**

We're living in pre-apocalyptic times, and our greatest concern is for lost souls. Today is the day to reach them, for Christ may come for us before the next sunrise.

Perhaps today is the day for you to reach out to someone you've been planning to lead to the Lord. We can't do tomorrow's work today any more than we can move backward in time to reverse yesterday's failures. The Lord assigns our work in the present tense, distributes His grace in the present, and tells us, "Behold, now is the accepted time; behold, now is the day of salvation" (2 Corinthians 6:2).

When it comes to sharing your faith, you can decide right now to become more proactive. We're not responsible for results, but we are responsible for actions that can yield results. Call a friend today and invite them to church. Build a friendship with an unsaved friend. Interact with non-Christians, invite them to dinner, and show them the love and care of Christ. Offer to help others as opportunities arise, and whenever possible put good Christian materials in their hands. Suggest quality Christian radio stations, television programs, or books.

Tactfully share your faith in emails and social media. Pass along Bible verses in note cards, birthday cards, and Christmas cards. Ask others how you can pray for them, and do so faithfully. Share your personal experience, work on your testimony, and make sure you've memorized a simple plan for leading others to Christ.

Work in your church. Volunteer. Take part in children's ministries, knowing that many people make lifelong spiritual decisions as a child.

I'd also like to suggest you "talk prophecy" with people, for that subject intrigues almost everyone. People want to know what the Bible says about the End Times, the Last Days, the state of the world, the status of the Middle East, death, hell, and heaven.

When you're burdened for the lost, you never know how the Lord may use you.

Just ahead are the events of the book of Revelation—the Apocalypse. Perhaps today is the day to reach out, serving the Lord and sharing the Lord.

Is there any event that would preclude Christ's soon return?

Though we do not know the day or hour of Christ's appearing for His Church, we do know something very important: It could be today! Why do I say that? Because nothing remains on God's prophetic calendar except the unfolding of end-time events, beginning with the Rapture of the Church. Theologians call it the doctrine of *imminence*—the return of Christ is imminent, meaning it could happen at any moment.

Because this hope is central to the life of every Christian and must never be allowed to fade from our awareness, I hope you will meditate for just a moment on that truth. Today, if you belong to Jesus Christ, you could be caught up to meet Him in the air and be with Him forever (1 Thessalonians 4:13-18).

As long as modern churches have been holding revival meetings, the imminent return of Christ has been a reminder for Christians to be concerned about the work of preaching the Gospel—all in anticipation of the return of Jesus Christ.

Jesus warned the religious leaders of His day about their failure to understand "the signs of the times"—what God was doing in their own midst (Matthew 16:3). It is imperative that we base our hope and knowledge of the future on God's inerrant timetable in Scripture.

If "perhaps today" is the watchword for our generation, what do we need to know? There are three areas of our faith that are impacted by biblical prophecy: trusting God's plans instead of man's, living victoriously for Christ in the face of mounting obstacles, and reaching out to those who are living without hope in Christ.

The two most important events in human history are the first and second comings of Jesus Christ. Rightfully, we invest great effort in understanding His First Advent. But we must give no less attention to the Second Coming and its eternal ramifications—especially since this world-changing event could happen at any time.

Today, if you belong to Jesus Christ, you could be caught up to meet Him in the air and be with Him forever.

How can I become a difference maker in the world we live in today?

The Word of God give us assurance that we can make a difference in our world for Christ. Remember that:

- God has created us for a purpose (Psalm 139:13-16).

- God is at work in us to accomplish His purposes (Philippians 2:13).

- God will complete in us what He has called us to do (Philippians 1:6).

- God will use everything in our life to qualify us to serve Him (Romans 8:28).

- God increases our qualifications by allowing us to suffer (2 Corinthians 1:3-7).

- God never allows us to be separated from His love as His purpose for us unfolds (Romans 8:35-39).

- God uses His Word to create faith when we need it (Romans 10:17).

- God will open doors for us to walk through (Acts 16:6-10).

- God will use all that we've done for *Him* to make a difference in *us*—to conform us to the image of Christ (Romans 8:29).

What difference are you making for Him today? What difference could you make tomorrow?

Stand on God's promises and find your place—the place where you can make a difference for Him.

I want my life to be relevant—how can I put that into action?

In Jesus' day, it was common for everyone to have dusty feet and sandals. You couldn't leave your home and walk more than a few steps on a dirt road, in a field or on a mountainside, or even on a paved street in Jerusalem, without your feet becoming dusty. In fact, it was a matter of common courtesy and hospitality to provide a servant to wash the feet of guests as they entered a home (Luke 7:36-50; John 13:3-14).

Since most people don't walk on dusty streets today, that custom is no longer practiced. But it serves as a worthy metaphor for us. In biblical times, the only people who got their feet and sandals dusty were those who left the comfort and safety of their homes. Whether they were going to the market or going to minister, they had to leave home to do it. Likewise, if we are going to fulfill the Great Commission of Jesus Christ, we are going to have to leave home as well. It was Jesus who told a parable that contained these words: "Then the master said to the servant, 'Go out into the highways and hedges, and compel them to come in, that my house may be filled'" (Luke 14:23).

If ever there was an example of someone whose feet were dusty in the service of the Kingdom of God, it was Jesus Himself. In fact, He specifically said on one occasion that "Foxes have holes and birds of the air have nests, but the Son of Man has nowhere to lay His head" (Matthew 8:20). Jesus lived and ministered in the highways and byways of this world among people the religious elite of His day despised and ignored. He was often criticized for eating with "tax collectors and sinners" (Matthew 9:11).

But Jesus was also happy to socialize with those with whom He disagreed. The moment when a woman with a sinful past washed Jesus' feet with her own tears and hair was when He was eating a meal in the home of a Pharisee. Jesus made it clear that He came to help those who knew they needed help, not those who didn't (Mark 2:17). And in order to reach them, He lived His life where they were. He went to them—He didn't force them to come to Him.

John 20:21 summarizes what Jesus did and what He expects us to do also: "As the Father has sent Me, I also send you." Jesus lived His life with dusty feet because He lived in obedience to His Father. If our feet aren't equally "dusty," it calls into question our obedience to His command to "Go therefore and make disciples" (Matthew 28:19).

Commission

Go ye therefore, and teach all
nations, baptizing them in the name
of the Father, and of the Son, and
of the Holy Ghost.

MATTHEW 28:19, KJV

What shall I do as I live in these ever-changing and challenging days?

As world conditions worsen, Jesus said we shouldn't hang our heads in hopelessness or shake our heads in confusion. Instead, we should lift up our heads in expectation, for our redemption draws near (Luke 21:28). After Paul told the Thessalonians about the sudden return of Christ in the air for His people, he said, "Comfort one another with these words" (1 Thessalonians 4:18).

Our world is in a state of depression. Proverbs 12:25 states: "Anxiety in the heart of a man causes depression, but a good word makes it glad." Obviously there are times when medication is absolutely called for, but meditation is often better. When we visualize our Lord's return, we're treating our souls to a "good word."

Jesus told His worried disciples on His last night with them, "Let not your heart be troubled; you believe in God, believe also in Me. In My Father's house are many mansions. … I will come again and receive you to Myself" (John 14:1-3).

Try this experiment. One evening, sit down and watch television for an hour, focusing on a roundup of the world news. It'll be an hour filled with riots, war, politics, problems, budget deficits, serial killers, and natural disasters. Reflect on how you feel afterward.

The next night, turn off the television and study First and Second Thessalonians, two little books in the New Testament with much to say about the Lord's return. Read Paul's promise that God will give His anxious children rest "when the Lord Jesus is revealed from heaven with His mighty angels" (2 Thessalonians 1:7). After an hour of pondering the eight little chapters of the Thessalonian epistles, my guess is you'll have joy in your heart as you anticipate His return.

The study of the signs of the times isn't just for "Second Coming scholars." It's for every single Christian who loves His appearing. It's comprehensible and it's compelling and it will change your life. It is a practical subject with tangible benefits, and those who study it are happier, holier, healthier people. We can rightly consider it the greatest self-improvement course we can take, and the benefits are eternal.

During these challenging days, find out what the Bible has to say about the prophetic times, and learn to pray: *Even so, come, Lord Jesus!*

What are we to do as we wait for Christ's return?

Our calling is to spread the Gospel to the ends of the earth. When we're involved in missions, we're part of the greatest international enterprise on earth. We all have our work to do like crewmen on a ship, and each of us has our own gifts, talents, opportunities, and positions. When it comes to missions, nothing beats the spirit and determination of a crew committed to the Captain and determined to complete the voyage. The crew is the "ye" in the Great Commission. Jesus said, "Go ye into all the world, and preach the gospel to every creature" (Mark 16:15, KJV). The "ye" is *you* and *me*—it's us! You and I are called by God to take His cargo—the message of the cross—to the ends of the earth.

When you read the Great Commission, please don't think it applies to someone else—to preachers or evangelists or missionaries. It applies to each of us, to all God's children. This is the way Christianity spread in the book of Acts and in the days of the Early Church. That means we must be excited, eager, and available, filled with the wonder of what Christ has done for us. Our testimonies are simply the overflow of grateful hearts, and our soul-winning is the by-product of our enthusiasm for Christ and His Gospel.

According to the Bible, the Lord Jesus Christ wants to continue His ministry of evangelism through you. It's a matter of everyone's personal ministry, for the Bible says, "He who wins souls is wise" (Proverbs 11:30).

My desire is to stay dedicated to the Word of God. How do I stay true to that desire?

If you're dedicated to something, you're committed to it wholly and earnestly. You've found something that demands your life, your soul, your all. For Christians, that cause is Christ and His Word.

First, **read** the Word.

The apostle Paul exhorted us to give attention to reading, to exhortation, and to doctrine (1 Timothy 4:13). The book of Revelation promises, "Blessed is he who reads and those who hear the words of this prophecy" (Revelation 1:3). If you don't have a plan for reading the Bible, devise one for yourself today and start it at once.

Second, **study** the Bible. How marvelous that God gave us a Book large enough to contain all we need to know from Him, yet small enough to fit in our hands. The Bible says, "The works of the Lord are great, studied by all who have pleasure in them" (Psalm 111:2).

Third, **memorize** the Scripture. Job 22:22 says, "Lay up his words in your heart" (NIV). By memorizing a verse of Scripture, you're inscribing God's Word on your brain. It makes the Bible portable and allows the Scripture to transform your life by the renewing of your thoughts.

Fourth, **meditate** on God's Word. This is the forgotten habit of the Church. Encircled by radios, televisions, computers, and portable devices, we're seldom quiet long enough to meditate. But try mulling over a verse of Scripture during your morning shower, your daily commute, or before falling asleep at night. According to the Bible, this is the secret of success. Joshua 1:8 says this about God's Word, "You shall meditate in it day and night, that you may observe to do according to all that is written in it. For then you will make your way prosperous, and then you will have good success."

Fifth, it is important to **pray** the Scripture. After reading, studying, and perhaps memorizing a verse, turn it into a prayer for yourself or someone else. By doing that, you're bringing God's Word right back to Him. You're claiming it before His throne. You can do this with almost any passage. You undoubtedly know someone else who needs that prayer offered on his or her behalf. Find a verse, put your name on it, or that of someone else, and claim it in prayer.

But here's the important thing. We can read, study, memorize, meditate, and even pray the Scriptures; but unless we obey its words, it does no good.

Whenever you read a verse, ask: "Is there an action I need to take, a command I need to obey, a change I need to make, or an attitude I need to adopt?" Learn to read the Bible obediently.

Finally, dedication to the Word of God creates a desire to share your faith. As you fill your heart with God's Word, the overflow of God's love will be seen through your life and testimony. The world will then see—"Christ in you, the hope of glory" (Colossians 1:27).

How does the Great Commission apply to me?

The Great Commission of Christ is a corporate mission statement given to the Church as a whole (Matthew 28:19-20). The Church's mission is to make disciples of all the nations. But what is your part in that mission? What has God equipped and called you to do as part of the Body of Christ?

Shouldn't we, as Christians, be able to verbalize our spiritual mission in life? Shouldn't we also ask ourselves, "What spiritual business am I in?" and "How's business?" I think we should. But you can't answer the second of those questions without knowing the answer to the first. And you can't know the answer to the first without knowing your personal spiritual mission in life. Where is God calling you to be a light to the lost in your world? Each of us has a mission that we need to faithfully fulfill.

The urgency of our mission is real even though we do not know the time of Christ's return. Only God the Father knows when it will occur. All we can do is prepare ourselves for that day, and share the Good News of the Gospel whenever and wherever we have the opportunity, for the time is short. The Bible says that no one in either the natural world or the supernatural world knows when Jesus will return. But we can look to the signs around us and know that we need to be about our Father's business.

In Isaiah 6:8, we read these words, "Here am I! Send me." I want to encourage you, going forward, to use every day and hour wisely for Christ and His kingdom. Take a moment to reflect over your life, think about your opportunities, and rededicate yourself to His glory. It's not just your time He wants, but *you*—all your resources. Your time. Your place. Your voice. Your mark of influence. Your marching orders may begin with those five words, "Here am I! Send me."

> *The urgency of our mission is real even though we do not know the time of Christ's return.*

Why is it important to study prophecy?

Prophecy unlocks the puzzle for living today and offers:

Hope for the future! Reading God's prophecies is like reading the last page of a romantic novel and discovering that the guy gets the girl. Prophecy tells us Christ comes to rule and reign forever.

Confidence in the present! When you don't fear tomorrow, you can have confidence today. People are fearful because they don't know God's prophetic story.

Holiness in living! The sure knowledge of Christ's appearing is strong motivation for us to keep ourselves pure. What child is not on his best behavior knowing his parent will soon be home?

Reasons to share the Good News! Our world is full of confused and despairing people who are overwhelmed by the seemingly random nature of our chaotic world. Prophecy is good news for those who think all the news is bad.

Edification! Exhortation! Encouragement! The apostle Paul said that God gave prophets to the Church to build us up (edification), set us straight (exhortation), and keep us going (encouragement) (1 Corinthians 14:3). I can't think of anything our world needs more than these three benefits.

Can I count on you to become an activist in these last, tremulous days of history?

Because we have the puzzle box top and know where all the pieces fit, we should pick up our banners and signs and "take to the streets" with the Good News of God's prophetic Word.

Life can be like a puzzle until you take the pieces out of the box, arrange them according to God's prophetic panorama, and step back and take a fresh look. When you do that, the things most people worry about become pieces which complete the picture God has painted of the End Times. Instead of a puzzle, life becomes a panorama of God's truth and hope!

The Judge is before the door: he that cometh will come, and will not tarry: his reward is with him.

GEORGE WHITEFIELD

We are pressed on every side by troubles, but we are not crushed. We are perplexed, but not driven to despair. We are hunted down, but never abandoned by God. We get knocked down, but we are not destroyed. Through suffering, our bodies continue to share in the death of Jesus so that the life of Jesus may also be seen in our bodies. Yes, we live under constant danger of death because we serve Jesus, so that the life of Jesus will be evident in our dying bodies.

2 CORINTHIANS 4:8-11, NLT

Challenge

> **What should be my first step toward living with an eternal perspective and purpose?**

The first step is to do a checkup on what is most important to you. To see if you have an eternal perspective and purpose, take this quick test. As honestly as possible, answer these questions:

- Do I have the same excitement about my mansion in heaven as I do about fixing up my house on earth?

- What proportion of my time is spent keeping up with friends via social media compared to the time holding them up before the Lord in prayer?

- Am I more excited about spending ninety percent of my income on my own purposes or about the ten percent I'm able to give to the Lord?

- Am I as diligent in studying God's Word as I am in reading the latest gossip in the tabloids or on the Internet?

- Do I fall asleep thinking about the problems of earth or the promises of heaven?

How did you do? While taking care of temporal things is important, it should pale in comparison to the investments made for eternity. It's great to focus our energy on the goals and projects of every day, but don't forget Colossians 3:1-2: "Seek those things which are above, where Christ is, sitting at the right hand of God. Set your mind on things above, not on things on the earth."

As followers of the One seated in heaven, we have an obligation to help others look toward glory. We can never take our houses or trophies with us into eternity. Our most prized possessions will be boxed up and forgotten.

Those trinkets we've collected may end up at a flea market. Our money may be dispersed to others. But our life can point others to heaven. Our funds can help others hear the Gospel. Our words of witness can make a heaven-or-hell difference in the lives of those to whom the Lord leads us. Our church involvement can contribute to an eternal cause.

We should always be living with an eternal perspective and purpose.

"If you read history," observed C. S. Lewis, "you will find that the Christians who did most for the present world were precisely those who thought most of the next."[2]

That's what it means to see beyond this world. That's what happens when we live with an eternal purpose in mind.

[2] C. S. Lewis, *Mere Christianity* (New York: The Macmillan Company, 1943), 104.

> **I want to see revival in my world, where does it begin?**

Revival means "an improvement in the condition or strength," a "resurgence," a "restoration" of something that was already there. In spiritual terms, the essential idea is of a new surge of spiritual life, a life that is already present but is flickering, perhaps feebly. Revival is the return of something to its true nature and original purpose.

So when there is a revival, God's people return to what they are supposed to be anyway. They are revived and brought back to a place of fellowship with Him.

But why is revival necessary? Why is it that over and over again in the history of the Christian world, there have had to be movements of renewal and revival to keep God's church alive and well? Throughout biblical history and our times today, we see that when believers allow the culture or the circumstance they live in to encroach into their time with God, there is a need for renewal. We are not asking God to be revived. He needs no revival. It is God's people who need the revival. So periodically it becomes necessary for God to do a renewing and reviving work in the hearts of His children.

Do you know what happens when revival comes to your heart? You open the Book and it is like it is brand new. All of a sudden, you read the Scripture and it is like you have never read it before. God gives you a whole new appreciation of His Word. It is so easy, as believers, to get into the routine of reading the Bible or hearing it preached or listening to it online, and it is like a dead, cold exercise. But when the fire burns brightly inside you because you have been renewed by the Spirit of God, you open His Book and the words jump off the page. It is like it is brand new.

When does revival begin? How does it happen? Revival begins with a renewed devotion to God's Word. As God's people return to the study of God's Word, are praying, are convicted about sin, and are ready to follow God's leading, revival can begin in individual hearts. We can't orchestrate widespread, far-reaching revivals; that's God's work. But we can make sure our heart is constantly prepared for what He wants to do with and through us. We should be willing, ready, and waiting to do whatever the Lord impresses on our heart. God revives those who are ready to obey Him, whenever and wherever He bids us.

Second Chronicles 7:14 reminds us: "If My people who are called by My name will humble themselves; and pray and seek My face, and turn from their wicked ways, then I will hear from heaven, and will forgive their sin and heal their land."

He has work for you today. Ask God to revive your heart and your spirit—you can become part of His revival in the Last Days.

Salvation Is for Today

In Isaiah 55, we have an urgent biblical warning about salvation: "Seek the Lord while He may be found, call upon Him while He is near. Let the wicked forsake his way, and the unrighteous man his thoughts; let him return to the Lord … for He will abundantly pardon" (Isaiah 55:6-7). But the same chapter also stresses the urgency of sharing the Gospel with those needing Christ: "For as the rain comes down, and the snow from heaven … so shall My word be that goes forth from My mouth; it shall not return to Me void" (Isaiah 55:10-11).

If the Lord could come at any time, then He could come today. That's why today is the day of salvation. How sad to wait too long! When it comes to being saved—or to sharing the Gospel of salvation—today is the day to act. If you need Christ as your Savior, you can trust Him right now. In prayer, you can quietly and simply ask Him to forgive your sins and to change your life. You can acknowledge Him as your risen Redeemer and commit your life to Him right where you are.

You can have the light of Christ in your life— and regardless of the world we live in—you can have peace.

Jesus said to them, "A little while longer the light is with you. Walk while you have the light, lest darkness overtake you; he who walks in darkness does not know where he is going. While you have the light, believe in the light, that you may become sons of light .... I have come as a light into the world, that whoever believes in Me should not abide in darkness" (John 12:35-36, 46).

Share the light today!

Topical Index

A *Affliction,* 28

B *Body of Christ,* 48, 126, 183
Boldness/Courage, 6, 8, 22-23, 41, 87, 122

C *Character/Characteristics,* 21, 56, 66, 92, 99, 158-159
Christian Walk, 58-59, 66-67, 68-69, 72-73, 74-75, 78-79, 82-83, 90, 92, 100-101, 116-117, 118, 119-121, 130-131, 134, 141-142, 145, 199
Church, The, 13, 31, 33, 38, 127, 130, 133, 164, 180, 183, 187
Compassion, 9, 11, 18, 94-95, 98-99, 101, 116
Culture, 6, 8-9, 31, 42, 49, 130, 143

E *Encouragement,* 45, 42, 56, 84, 87, 94, 96-97, 115, 122-123, 133-134, 184, 187
Endure, 26, 28, 84-85, 125

Evangelism/Outreach,   18, 25-26, 45, 82-83, 86-87,
    94-95, 100-101, 108-109, 110, 112-113, 126, 161-
    162, 178, 193-194

F   *Faith, Faithful,*   6, 8-9, 10, 12-13, 14, 22-29, 35, 37,
    39, 42-43, 44, 46, 53, 54, 59, 60, 62, 68-69, 71, 84-
    85, 87-88, 93, 98-99, 103, 106, 108, 112, 122-123,
    125, 132, 135, 136-137, 141-142, 145, 149, 151,
    155- 156, 161-162, 165, 168, 182, 184

G   *Good News,*   110-111, 184, 187, 188
    Gospel,   25, 26, 31, 43, 90, 101, 110, 123, 126-127,
    136, 143, 144-145, 154, 165, 177-178, 184, 194,
    199

    Great Commission, The,   136, 170, 177, 183
    Guidance,   9, 14, 49, 58-59, 74, 134

H   *Hope,*   7, 43, 143-145, 164-165, 174, 182, 186, 188

L   *Last Days,*   4, 6, 12, 19, 20, 27, 30, 112, 163, 197

M   *Mission,*   10, 11, 110, 126, 155-157, 177, 183-185

P   *Prayer/Praying,*   8, 10, 14, 34-35, 46, 58, 67, 73,
    76-77, 93, 109, 114-115, 122, 134, 141-142, 181,
    192, 199
    Promises,   13, 24, 46, 54, 69, 82, 101, 102, 158-160,
    168, 193

Prophecy/Future Events, 6-7, 10, 30, 32, 139, 153, 154, 163, 165, 179, 186-187

Purpose, 14, 33, 35-38, 57-58, 73, 77, 99, 112, 160, 167-168, 192, 194-195

R *Relationships,* 51, 62, 66, 75, 82, 125, 146

Resurrection, 96

Revival, 195-197

S *Salvation,* 199-200

Satan, 33-39, 112, 152

Sin/Temptation, 37, 51, 59, 67, 69, 71, 73, 78-79, 81, 90, 92, 117-119, 120-121, 131, 134, 145, 170-171, 197, 199

Spiritual Warfare, 33-34

Strength, 9, 19, 24, 39, 42, 59, 69, 76-77, 79, 80-81, 84, 103, 133, 159, 195

T *Trials/Persecution,* 6, 26, 31, 54, 68, 84-85, 86, 102

Tribulation, 30, 134

Trust/Trusting, 27-2942-43, 44, 46-47, 54, 68, 77, 86-87, 101, 103, 165, 199

W *Wisdom,* 14, 20, 57, 90, 92-93, 102, 110, 142 156, 178, 184

Witness, 10, 25, 26, 31, 45, 83, 100-101, 108, 110, 116-117, 136, 194

World, The, 12, 16, 18, 25, 51-52, 56-57, 63, 101, 155, 200

Additional

Resources

The Book of Signs

The Bible tells us to watch out for the signs in our world that will foreshadow the End Times. In *The Book of Signs*, Dr. Jeremiah takes an in-depth look at the prophecies in Scripture and how they correlate with the events of our time. This book will help you grow in your knowledge of biblical prophecy and give you renewed confidence in the future God has planned for us.

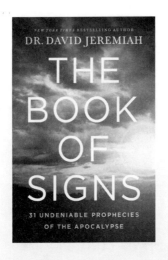

Answers to Questions About Prophecy

Prophecy can often be mysterious, which can be confusing for some, but it is necessary to understand the events that are to come. In this book, Dr. Jeremiah answers over sixty questions about prophecy, including the topics of the Rapture, the Tribulation, and the Second Coming. This book is the perfect resource for those who are just beginning their journey into prophecy and for those who are well-versed in the Scriptures.

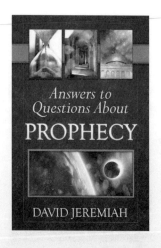

Answers to Questions About
PROPHECY

DAVID JEREMIAH

800-947-1993 | www.DavidJeremiah.org

The Handwriting on the Wall

In *The Handwriting on the Wall*, Dr. Jeremiah shows how an understanding of prophecy leads to dynamic living in our culture today. By studying the book of Daniel and the far-reaching significance of the events within it, you will grow in your ability to live faithfully today and to anticipate the future confidently.

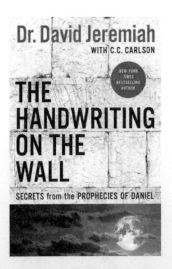

Agents of Babylon

Throughout history, Babylon has been a symbol of the world's worst evils, and nowhere in the Bible do we get a more vivid picture of the malevolent nature of Babylon than the book of Daniel. In *Agents of Babylon*, you will become acquainted with the most prominent players in the book of Daniel—kings and rulers, royal counselors, animals, angels both good and evil, and inanimate objects like trees and statues. Through this study you will learn why Daniel's devotion to prayer is as critical today as it was in his time.

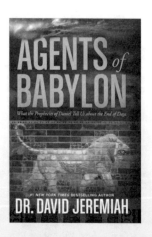

People Are Asking … Is This the End?

With jarring headlines and rapid cultural changes, few would dispute that the pace at which things are currently changing is unprecedented. No one can afford to ignore these warnings, but all can better understand the greater story and the role we each play in this changing world. From prophetic clues in Scripture to an understanding of the power of Christ in all believers, this book directs you on a clear path forward.

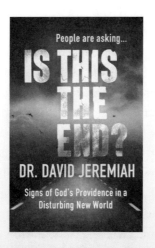

About David Jeremiah

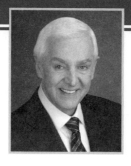

David Jeremiah is the founder of Turning Point for God, an international broadcast ministry committed to providing Christians with sound Bible teaching through radio and television, the Internet, live events, and resource materials and books. He is the author of more than fifty books including *A Life Beyond Amazing*, *The Book of Signs*, and *Overcomer*. David serves as senior pastor of Shadow Mountain Community Church in San Diego, California, where he resides with his wife, Donna. They have four grown children and twelve grandchildren.